Practice

Islamic Society in Practice

Carolyn Fluehr-Lobban

University Press of Florida

Gainesville Tallahassee Miami Boca Raton
Pensacola Orlando Tampa Jacksonville

Library of Congress Cataloging-in-Publication Data

Fluehr-Lobban, Carolyn.
    Islamic society in practice / Carolyn Fluehr-Lobban.
        p. cm.
    Includes bibliographical references (p. 181) and index.
    ISBN 0-8130-1305-4. — ISBN 0-8130-1319-4 (pbk.)
        1. Islam—Africa, North.   2. Islam—Sudan.   3. Islam—Egypt.   4. Islam—Tunisia.
    5. Africa, North—Religious life and customs.   6. Sudan—Religious life and customs.
    7. Egypt—Religious life and customs.   8. Tunisia—Religious life and customs.
    BP64.A4N6423   1994   94-13713
    297'.0962—dc20

99   98   6   5   4

Photo on dedication page: the author (*right*) and her mother in Suez, Egypt.

The University Press of Florida is the scholarly publishing agency for the State University System of Florida, comprised of Florida A & M University, Florida Atlantic University, Florida International University, Florida State University, University of Central Florida, University of Florida, University of North Florida, University of South Florida, and University of West Florida.

University Press of Florida
15 Northwest 15th Street
Gainesville, FL 32611

For my mother, Anne Wolsonovich Fluehr, whose keen eye and love of geography, history, and travel have always been an inspiration

Contents

Illustrations

Acknowledgments

This book is both scholarly and personal. For its academic content I accept and readily bear full accountability. However, the personal side of this book is filled with the richness of family, warm memories of hospitality and both good and bad times shared in the field, and two decades of teaching at Rhode Island College, all of which have helped greatly to sharpen my view of self and the other.

First of all to my mother, Anne Wolsonovich Fluehr, to whom this book is dedicated, I express my deep gratitude for giving me a love of geography and travel. Her enthusiasm for life, and for the fun of observing its small and great events, from her journalistic and very human viewpoint, has been an inspiration. On two occasions she joined in anthropological research adventures in Egypt. And each time we were in the field, as husband and wife or a family of four, it was her newsy letters from home that kept us in touch with American culture as we were actively absorbing parts of Muslim and Arab culture.

Richard, my husband and fellow anthropologist, and I have shared research experiences in Khartoum, Cairo, and Tunis over two decades totaling over five years' residence, first as a newly married couple and later as a real "family" (by Middle East standards) with our daughters, Josina and Nichola. We have lived together in Khartoum (in 1970–72 and in 1979–80), in Cairo (1982–83), and in Tunis (1990), and we have shared fully the intellectual and emotional side of anthropological fieldwork. Our exchanges and mutual observations over the years in three different countries have established a rich foundation for the content and objectives of this book.

Our daughters, Josina and Nichola ("Nicki"), were at first small companions to their parents' research and travel interests, but over the years, with three separate "fieldwork" experiences for Josina and two for Nicki, they have been enthusiastic supporters and all around good sports. We have promised Josina, in her last years in high school, that we will not take her out of the country again so that she can graduate with her friends. Nicki is still eager to go abroad, but we plan to respect her adolescence too. Having these children with us at various stages of their lives has proved an enormous benefit and has always given us a kids' point of view to ponder and include. To all of these family members, I express loving acknowledgment and gratitude.

To my students over the past two decades of teaching at Rhode Island College, I want to express a special thank-you. I thank those students who expressed an honest anger that they had not been better educated about the history and culture of the Arab and Islamic world, and who were motivated to replace ignorance with knowledge. I thank those students who wanted to be able to read the newspaper better, or sort out the biases of the electronic media's reporting on Islam and the Arab world, especially the adult, returning students with whom we are blessed at Rhode Island College. For the students who wanted to know more about the everyday life of Muslims, their joys, hopes, fears, in short, their humanity, I say thank you for affirming the validity of this approach. And even to the students who formed a part of that captive audience required to take a non-Western course, I say thanks for challenging me to make this an interesting subject to those operating more from compulsion than from choice.

To the many friends and acquaintances made over the years, first in the Sudan, and later in Egypt and Tunisia, I express the fondest thank-you. It was their patience, kindness and acceptance of us that kept us coming back. There are too many names to list, but each is a precious memory.

Finally, I wish to express my gratitude to Robert Tidwell who has prepared the index for this book and to Dr. Youssef Hitti, who assisted me with Arabic transliteration in preparation of the Glossary of Arabic Terms and Names in the book (it is our mutual hope that a more standardized form of Arabic transliteration will become more widely used and accepted in American English).

1

Introduction

The complicated relations and associated tension between the West and Christianity and the Arab world and Islam are deeply rooted in history and have been marked by political and cultural struggles often waged in the name of religion. The past two decades, especially, have reawakened this tension and struggle between the West and the Arab-Muslim worlds with the dramatic events of the 1979 popular Islamic revolution in Iran; the assassination of the West's most charismatic Arab ally, Anwar al-Sādāt, in 1981; the taking of Western hostages in the context of the Lebanese civil war; the uprising of Palestinians in Israel; and the riveted attention of the West during the brief period of the Gulf War of 1990. The first three events have much to do with expressions of Islamic revival, whereas the last two bear a relationship to secular and Arab nationalist politics. Many in the West do not make such fine distinctions between Islamic revival and Arab nationalist politics in the Middle East and Muslim worlds and easily gloss over them with more facile generalizations and stereotypes that associate Islam with terrorism and Arab politics with an automatic anti-Western bias. As Edward Said has pointed out, for the general public in Europe and America today, Islam is news of a particularly unpleasant sort. Islam is perceived as a threat to Western civilization (1981: 136).

Although revived or militant Islamic movements have captured the most recent attention of the West in recent years, the majority of the world's nearly one billion Muslims stand outside of these events. And perhaps the most outstanding features of the Gulf war were the Arab alliance with the United States and its allies and the isolation of some Arab nationalists, such as Saddam Hussein and other Iraqi allies. The vast bulk of the Muslim population is not Arab and lives outside of the Middle East in nations that stretch from Malaysia, Indonesia, and Central Asia through the Middle East to major parts of the African continent

1

and even to a growing community in North America. While all are part of the world's community of Muslims, the *Umma,* each region has distinctive historical ties to the spread of Islam, and cultural and linguistic diversity is the norm, rather than the exception. The faith of Islam is a basic unifier, as is the Arabic language, valued by all Muslims because it was the language in which the Holy Book, the Qur'ān, was revealed to Muhammad nearly six centuries after the introduction of Christianity. Islam has been a powerful unifier because its theology has been, perhaps, less subject to the doctrinal disputes that Christianity has witnessed, and because its teachings blend religious, moral, and social practice into an indivisible whole for the believer-practitioner.

This Islam, as lived and practiced in everyday life and society, is the focus of this book. My goal in this book is to bring out the human dimension of a region and a cultural tradition that have been pigeonholed, stereotyped, and maligned, on the one hand, and simplified and romanticized, on the other. The book is an effort to get behind the headlines that have focused on war, conflict, terrorism, and fanaticism and to make accessible to a Western audience the lives of the everyday people of the Arab and Muslim worlds.

The major contours of the book are taken from an anthropologist's perspective, derived from five years of residence and research in three different Muslim countries. Its view is popular, in the sense that it derives from people, from the grass roots, from lives lived and observed. The observer is a Western woman whose view spans more than two decades, who first lived in the Sudan with her husband, later returned to the Sudan with one daughter, resided and researched in Egypt with a family grown to four, and, most recently, lived and worked in the Maghrib nation of Tunisia with her husband and two daughters, all a bit older. The years during which formal research was conducted, and during which in many ways the more important informal observations and reflections upon Muslim society were made, span the decades 1970–90. These were important years of dynamic change for the Arab and Muslim worlds and of self-examination and critical evaluation for the West's role in these regions. In my personal life, these decades took me from my mid-twenties to my mid-forties, from life as an anthropology graduate student to one as a tenured full professor in the discipline.

Anthropological studies of the Middle East and North Africa, as Ernest Gellner (1981) has observed, are generally approached "from below"; they are generally not rooted in texts and the analysis of records and documents. They may occasionally utilize textual sources, but these are often supplemental to what has been witnessed or experienced first-hand. The basic anthropological method of participant observation pre-supposes long-term stays, the ability to conduct research in the local language or dialect, and residence with the people studied. Research is often not predictable, and the best insights can occur in the interstices, where they are least expected. There is not the comfort or security of texts, of documents viewed and reviewed, or perhaps photocopied for later viewing, in libraries or research institutes; there is not the certainty of the written word that can be quoted and cited, but only the uncertainty of self and of self in relation to others, of life lived and observed in its untidy, ever-changing, day-to-day dynamic.

I recall with some embarrassment even today an exchange that took place early in my fieldwork in the Sudan when I was still learning conversational Arabic. Several young Sudanese women were questioning me about American culture and religion, when one of them broke in with the question, "Do you eat pork?" "Oh, not very often", was my response, proud that I could express a degree of frequency between always and not at all, whereupon a hushed silence replaced the banter that had been under way. I realized that I had made a terrible error in revealing this unclean, unacceptable pork eating behavior to them. Red-faced, I tried to turn the conversation to another subject, but I was unsuccessful as they looked at me now not just as an oddity but as an unhygienic one. It is this sort of experience that makes an indelible impression about the deep feelings associated with a food taboo in society, feelings that are not replicable for a researcher working with a text or document.

There is an important body of literature in the West that has been associated with the study of the Islamic faith and its textual sources: Orientalism. Orientalism can be defined most simply as the study of the East by the West. Orientalist scholars have examined the holy books of Islam: the Qur'ān, the books of Ḥadīth about what the Prophet is reported to have said and done in his lifetime, the books interpreting the religious law called the Sharī'a, and the opinions of many of the famous Muslim scholars on religious subjects. Orientalism as a scholarly body of literature dates from the time of Napoleon in Egypt; he brought teams of scholars with his military expedition, and it enjoyed its heyday during the decades of European colonial rule.

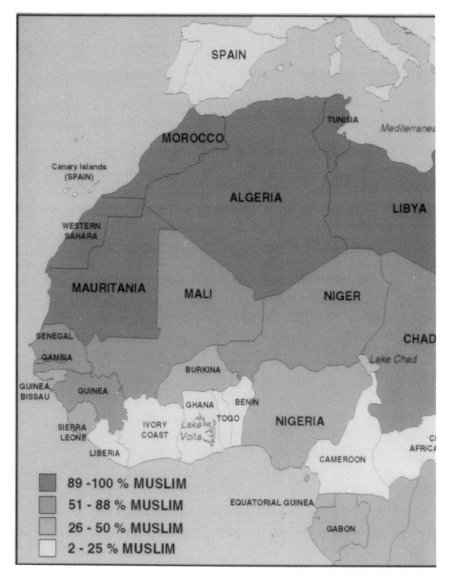

Fig. 1. Percent of Muslim peoples in Southwest Asia and North Africa. Developed by Richard Grant.

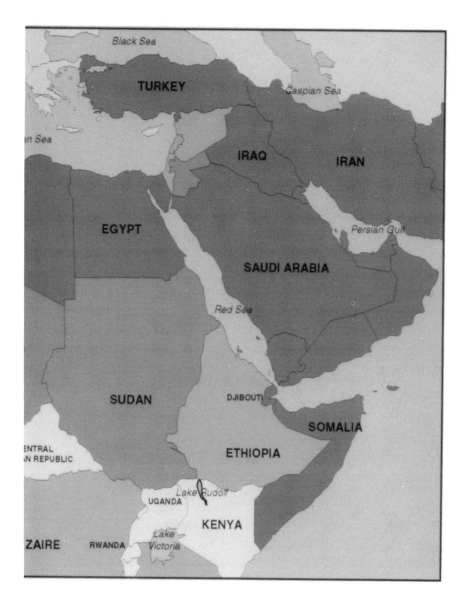

At the same time that the Orientalists have served to introduce Islam to the West, they have also introduced or carried forward a number of misconceptions about Islam and Muslims. One of the most fundamental errors made was the reference to the religion of Islam as Mohammedanism; by doing so they elevated the Prophet Muhammad to the status of deity, like Jesus Christ, for which the religion of Christianity is named. Muhammad was a man and the Messenger of Islam (*Rasūl Allāh*), last of the great prophets of the Abrahamic tradition in the Middle East, but not God nor a son of God. The term *Mohammedanism* came into the West and became a standard reference for the religion in English throughout the contact and colonial periods. It began to disappear only as a postcolonial literature and consciousness began to replace the Orientalist tradition in the various Muslim nations of Africa and Asia. Early Orientalist artists, such as Jean-Léon Gérôme, Eugène Delacroix, August Reno, J. F. Lewis, and David Roberts, created beautiful, romanticized paintings of mosques, bazaars, and "Arab" festivals, and they were especially fascinated by the harem and by conditions of "Oriental" slavery, certainly different from the images of plantation slavery in the New World. Whereas no Muslim would call himself or herself a Mohammedan, the use of the term reflects the Orientalist approach that relied on relatively superficial contacts with people and was occupied with its own construction of Oriental reality.

Another Orientalist view that created an offense against the religion of Islam was the idea that the Qur'ān, which Muslims believe to be the revealed word of God, was written by Muhammad. This assertion has been posed as a great puzzle by the Orientalists since Muhammad was not literate enough to produce a work that sets the standard for the rich and complex Arabic language. It is perhaps this "puzzle" that Salman Rushdie's *Satanic Verses* attempts to resolve; this work of fiction posits the view that the Qur'ān was dictated to Muhammad by Satan. Highly controversial, this work was defended as artistic freedom in the West, but was condemned (to the point of a death sentence *fatwa* issued by Ayatollah Khomenei and renewed by his successors) and reviled in the Muslim world as the latest example of the West's ignorance and intolerance of Islam. Salman Rushdie was raised as a Muslim, and although both he and his work published in the West have been condemned in Iran, this fatwa has not been supported by the larger Muslim community of scholars.

Revision of these earlier views has fallen to Arab critics of the Orientalists, A. L. Tibawi, Anour Abdel Malik and Edward Said, but others have joined this critical scholarship to note the errors, the arrogance, and the subjectivity of this viewpoint known as Orientalism (Hussain, Olson, Qureshi, 1984; Spaulding and Kapteijns, 1991). This critique, made especially popular and accessible by Edward Said, has entered mainstream Western discourse, and a point of view that is critical of Orientalism is at least recognized and may be cited when a more balanced view is sought.

More recent studies by Western, post-Orientalist historians have sought to comprehend the development of Arab and Muslim society more on its own terms than as a consequence of or a reaction to events in Western history (Hourani 1991). Likewise, an increasing number of firsthand anthropological accounts of life as lived by Arabs and Muslims in various geographical and historical contexts have helped to correct the literature regarding previous Orientalist inventions of Islamic society. The interpretations presented in many of these works are incorporated into this present text, which itself seeks to present an alternative view to that of Orientalism.

Other, more formal studies of the Islamic faith by Muslims in English, such as works by Fazlur Rahman and Sayed Hossein Nasr, are valued aids in studying Islam, as are more recent, basic introductions to the religion intended for a general, Western audience, such as John Esposito's *Islam the Straight Path*.

In sum, these works constitute a new body of knowledge that permits us in the West to have access to a more objective understanding of the religion of Islam and the society it invokes and promotes.

The Experience of Fieldwork 1970–1990: Shaping the Author's View

Anthropologists employ participant observation in their studies of non-Western and Western cultures, which as already noted presumes long term residence and language acquisition in the culture being studied. Familiarity with everyday life is a given, and anthropologists quickly learn that they often have unusual mobility in other peoples' societies.

Learning Arabic in 1968 and 1969 in the United States, in our case in Chicago, was not easy. Generally speaking, only a generation ago universities did not teach conversational Arabic, or what is known as literary modern standard Arabic. This has changed greatly today due to the increase in interest in Arab-Muslim societies, but two decades ago the formal study of the Arabic language was available mainly to the linguist and the religious specialist. Richard and I realized that this skill would have to be acquired in the field.

Sudan and Egypt: 1970–84

When we arrived in Khartoum for the first time in 1970, we had only had some basic training in Arabic letters and sounds, but little conversational ability. Since so much of anthropological fieldwork is information acquired by listening and observing, learning Arabic by ear became a natural extension of that process. There are obvious advantages to learning a language in its natural setting, and the assuredness about the contextual use of expressions and phrases that this conveys is one that has served many an anthropological insight. Often recalling a phrase or word as being used in a particular mood to convey a special meaning is an excellent means of analyzing cultural values. 'Ayb (Shame) is such a powerful word-expression with many contextual usages. It can be used to reprimand a child or to criticize a politician; it can be used by a judge reproaching some shameful adult behavior, and it is a type of divorce due to impotence in a man. Absorbing the contextual use of language aids in understanding both the nuances of language and of culture.

The disadvantage of learning a language by ear is that literacy in the language lags behind, and the act of conversation and human interaction surpasses the desire or ability to read the newspaper, for example. We frequently took in the news of the world by ear, as conversational use of the language overtook its literary usage.

After some initial study of Arabic grammar and linguistic structure, Richard and I settled into a life where English was primarily used between us at home and Arabic was used for public discourse. This was a process, we soon realized, that was much like that of a baby learning to make linguistic sense of its world. Thus we made many silly mistakes in the initial phase of learning conversational, colloquial Sudanese Arabic. For example, the Arabic words for liver (kibda), cheese (jibna) and butter (zibda), presented for us a special challenge because of their similarity to our relatively untutored ears; so we often mistakenly asked for one when we meant the other. Likewise, the different forms of a word, from the singular to the dual or to the plural were a challenge and an amusement to us; *finjān* (one cup) became *finjanain* (two cups) and then was altered further to *fanajīn* for three of more cups, only to revert to the singular after ten. *Bayt* (one house) was easily transformed to *baytain* (two houses), but we frequently had to guess what the proper plural form would be, in this case, *Bayoot*. Occasionally, the role of teacher and student were exchanged: if an English-speaking Sudanese would mispronounce "bort" (port) or "Bepsi" (Pepsi), due to the lack of the consonant "p" in Arabic, we could make the gentle correction. Generally, our language acquisition was accomplished in pleasant company with good times, due to the patience and hospitality of our hosts. After six months, when we had the occasion to meet the then President of the Sudan, Ja'afar al-Numayri, we were pleased to have been able to conduct that brief conversation entirely in Arabic.

By this time we had been given Sudanese names which were used in introducing us, and these names never failed to make an impression and helped people to remember us by a familiar name. My name, Mihera bint Abboud, was selected from 19th century history, the name of a Shayqiya woman who exhorted the hesitating men of her group to resist the invading Turco-Egyptian armies by riding ahead of them on camel back and ululating, what Sudanese call the *zaghareet*, "ayoo-yoo-yooo". This story never failed to excite me and stir my imagination and I was proud to bear the name of this genuine Sudanese heroine. Richard, my husband, was given the name of one of the great nationalist leaders of the 1924 "White Flag" rebellion against British imperialism, Abd al-Fadil Al-Maz, a name that was symbolically important since this fallen hero was a southern patriot from the days when northerners and southerners fought together against the common foe of colonialism, rather than fighting each other.

In the Sudan, as well as in Egypt and Tunisia, words and phrases have developed in the local dialect as a special way of expressing cultural values. The Egyptians have a more formal and hierarchical approach to casual contact with strangers or foreigners, and the special Turkish-derived "Effendum, Effendi" (Madam and Sir), is common. Much of my own language acquisition has been in the company of women with whom I have spent the greatest amount of social time. I thus learned to greet another woman with the more familiar, "Izzayik", or "Kaf al-hāl?" (How are you or how are things?), rather than the more formal "Essalaam alay kum" (Peace be upon you) that men would use. More recently, within the context of a revived Islam, both sexes are tending to use the more formal Muslim greeting.

In terms of housing arrangements, over the years we have emphasized a desire to be a part of community life. That approach has taken us from life on a houseboat on the Blue Nile in Khartoum, to residence with families when accommodation was problematical, to renting of apartments in the suburbs, or within the city's bustling market area, to living near the main transportation lines in the cities of Tunis and Cairo, since we most frequently relied on public transportation. The advantage to this, with research conducted within communities, is that of being in daily touch with life as lived by people. Conversations overheard on the tram to town, complaints about government corruption or inefficiency, working women discussing their problems at the butcher's, waiting in line at 5:00 AM for bread, all add up to powerful and lasting impressions, an immensely rich, and constantly stimulating experience.

Although it may have been difficult at times to be American nationals, as in Sudan during the Vietnam war in the early 1970's, or in Tunisia during the period just before the Gulf war, we never experienced, directly, any anti-Americanism. Perhaps our language ability in Arabic offset the potential critical remark, but more often we were praised, far beyond our real ability, for our fluency in Arabic. The fact is that few Westerners who have come to parts of the Arabic-speaking world as travelers or tourists speak Arabic, and the utter amazement with which we would be greeted was frequently followed by a barrage of questions as to whether we were of Arabic origin, or were very clever at languages, or, half-serious jokes about being spies. Why else would one bother to learn Arabic, a language they believe is devalued by Westerners, and in Tunisia is even devalued by many of the westernized Tunisian business and professional class. The possibility that we were merely curious, sincere people with a genuine interest in their culture and history was sometimes difficult to convey at first meeting.

Having children in the field has made a great difference. At first we were just a couple as graduate students in Sudan in 1970–1972, returning to the Sudan in 1975 still childless added fuel to the serious doubts, apparently, that many had about our truly being married. But returning in 1979 with a lovely, red-headed two and a half year old daughter was greeted with joy and a newfound legitimacy for us as a family. The

The author and her daughters with their Egyptian extended family.

experience of a young child in a predominantly Muslim society added a fresh perspective for us. First, on the matter of language, Josina was just beginning to speak English when we took her to Khartoum, so when we began to use Arabic on a regular basis, she took understandable offense. This came of some necessity since we were unable at the time to find separate accommodation and needed to live with the family of a friend of ours. While we used English among ourselves, most daily conversation was in Arabic, so in defense our daughter invented her own gibberish language that only she and her stuffed animals could understand.

Once we were established in our own flat in the central "Suq al-Arabi" area, Josina became adept at mimicking particular details of everyday life that she had observed on the street from our balcony, or in the process of moving about with her parents. She would imitate the Sudanese woman's "thobe" by placing her blanket over her head with a corner held between her teeth, as she had seen women do when riding on public transportation. One day she amazed us by bringing out to the living room floor area a bath towel, arranging it carefully and performing perfectly all of the motions of Muslim prayer, without the words. Where had she learned this, we wondered. Apparently she had observed from our balcony the local merchants praying together in the late afternoon before the shops opened for the evening.

She absorbed a great deal more about the practice of Islam in daily life without special instruction by just being a child trying to understand her surroundings. Hearing the call to prayer early each morning at sunrise and drifting back to sleep for a little while longer, hearing it another four times during the day from our home or while out walking made an impression, and our daughter would cup her ears, in the manner of the muezzin she had seen on television, and call out, "Allahu Hapgar". "No, No", we would say, *"Allahu Akbar"* ("God is great"), and she would repeat her first version that she had learned to say by herself.

The generosity that an egalitarian society like Sudan engenders is a value that is highly recognized and praised in Islamic society as well. Sharing is an expected part of being Muslim, especially with those less fortunate. The growing number of poor, homeless people on the streets of major cities is made more shameful and pitiable due to the continued strength of the value of extended familial bonds. A homeless person suggests no family to help out and makes a sad situation even worse. Offering some spare money to such persons is a good act and Josina would beg us to give her some coins to give to the street people. Her small act of generosity was often met with approving smiles or outright verbal praise from strangers and passersby. Frequently, when making a small purchase, such as candy or chewing gum, Josina would offer a piece of the newly purchased item to the salesperson with the usual invitation, "Itfadl", thinking that she was doing the right thing culturally, and, appropriately, most salespeople would accept with a broad appreciative smile.

Josina, at two and a half to three and a half years of age, had already assimilated enough American culture, before her time spent in Sudan, that she experienced a certain amount of culture shock. She did not accept the sexual segregation of her parents when visiting friends, and initially tried to get her Mommy to sit with Daddy and his friends. After repeated failures, she learned the rules of this cultural tradition, almost too well, and would enforce the rule strictly when guests came to call at our flat. Women, she would insist, must go into the bedroom to visit, while the men should stay in the living room.

She also resisted learning the language that her parents had suddenly shifted to just as she was beginning to master some basic English. Although she came to have the ability to follow a conversation pretty well, she often refused to perform on command to "say hello in Arabic", or "say good-bye". Her hidden talent was displayed one day when, having refused to greet some strangers on the street who had stopped to admire her red hair, and who remarked that she was as sweet as sugar, she shot back in perfect Arabic, "I'm not sugar, I'm hot pepper!"

Some years later, we brought our two children to Cairo, our younger daughter being just one year old at the time and just beginning to learn language and culture. Rather than experiencing some measure of culture shock, which her sister had earlier in Sudan, and which presumes a foundation of prior cultural learning, we had a child with basic motor skills ready and eager for language and behavioral training. This space was filled with everyday speech and mannerisms of the Egyptians with whom we lived and the grandfatherly cook, Hafez, who took a special interest in her nutrition and proper education. She began to speak Arabic at the same time as English, and did not make much differentiation between the two. "No!" seemed to have twice the impact if uttered in both languages, and the first full sentences were peppered with Arabic nouns and English verbs. Some important words started in Arabic and remained as a basic part of her vocabulary for a long time after our return, emotion-laden words, like "futa" for her special blanket, and the personal pronoun *Ana* (I) for self-identification.

It was Hafez who first noted that Nichola regularly sang after a meal once her stomach was full, a personal trait that continues to this day. It was with Hafez in the kitchen that she was able to observe the boy's elementary school, with its three sessions daily, and the more devout among them praying in the small mosque just below our window. She too learned the basic motions of prayer in this fashion, and would try to mimic the call to prayer, only this time she had a native speaker to correct her and train her properly, "Allahu Akbar", "God is great". Years later, when Nichola entered the great Blue Mosque on a trip to Istanbul, she pleaded to stay longer after the tour, to sit and be quiet, to watch the faithful at prayer, and to absorb the serene ambience. A spiritual sense was awakened in her, perhaps evoked by a distant memory of her early childhood in Cairo.

Nichola and her sister were taught only to use Arabic on the street and for every little treasure they wanted to purchase, the transaction would have to be carried out in Arabic. "I want a lollipop" (*"Ana 'owza bassassa"*) was the first and perhaps most frequently used sentence by Nichola. She would also beg for candy from our neighbor downstairs.

"Hellāwa" ("something sweet"), she would greet Umm Mohammed, instead of a more proper "Hello", thus her language learning seemed utterly opportunistic.

Her name, Nichola, is very similar to a well-known Greek boy's name, Nicola, so our little daughter was often taken for a little boy, since she did not have the customary ear piercing at an early age. Upon meeting her and learning her name, most Egyptians would remark what a handsome boy, to which Nichola learned a number of choice retorts. "No, I'm a girl", *"Bint, mush welad!"* Appropriate hand gestures went along the words, hand upraised. palm outward, moving it back and forth as in the American wave good-bye, but signaling "No, absolutely not a boy!" This particularly undesired form of public attention was an excellent inducement to wear a dress out of doors, instead of the more usual American-style, comfortable overalls.

Josina by now was five years of age, and spent her kindergarten and first grade school years at Cairo American College, an international school. There they taught Arabic twice a week, and took field trips to mosques which are open to the general public and to non-Muslims in Egypt, unlike our experiences in Tunisia and Sudan. Josina also went to the Pyramids for field trips and learned that there is no riddle to the Sphinx except how to save it from the devastating effects of 20th century pollution.

Tunisia: 1990

Our next opportunity to travel and live in northern Africa came when the girls were 13 years and 9 years, respectively. By this time they were seasoned travellers, and were accustomed to the culture, language and food differences, but were also more established Americans, having spent an intervening seven years back home in Rhode Island. They added to their knowledge of Arabic quite a bit of French, since Tunisia is strongly bilingual, especially in the urban areas.

In the intervening years we had also continued to teach courses on a regular basis dealing with the Middle East and Islam, and derived the benefit of working with sincere students eager to fill gaps in their traditional learning, and replace information with misinformation. Over the years we have benefitted enormously from our students' interest and positive response to, not only our formal studies in the region, but their powerful interest in the experiences we have had living in Middle Eastern and Muslim cultures. They have shown great enthusiasm not only in stories and slides but also physical, tactile and sensual objects from the region, such as clothing, perfumes, examples of Arabic calligraphy, music, children's books and learning boards (called *loh*), local money, good luck amulets, such as the "hand of Fāṭima" and "evil eye" symbols, and a host of other ephemera associated with the daily lives of the people we studied. This has encouraged us over the years to bring more such items back for use in the classroom. Also, more subtly, our own understanding and insight into the culture of "the other", and our own culture, was deepening in this process of living abroad and returning and then reflecting upon the experience for the purpose of teaching and communicating with Americans. The result is more one of interpretation than direct translation of cultural ideas and practice. This sincere interest displayed by our students and the general public, motivated by an effort to correct the lack of general education about the region and its peoples, is in a very important way the inspiration for this book.

Living in a home near to a local market and public transportation made our comings and goings frequent and much observed, so that within a short period of time we were known as the Americans who can speak Arabic and French (my husband, Richard, and daughter, Josina possess some conversational fluency). Few American families visit Tunisia or live there, except for diplomatic personnel, so we were something of a curiosity. The fact that I had to rely on Arabic and could not use French for everyday affairs was a source of discomfort or disbelief to many sales or business persons. Why would a "European" know Arabic and not French? The Islamist activists that I came to know later were not uncomfortable, but were very pleased that I used only Arabic and made exceptions for my Sudanese-Egyptian accent while they assisted me with the local Tunisian dialect. This was, for me, an important lesson in the powerful legacy of French colonialism, as language is a critical shaper of world view, and contextually in Tunisia, French is the language of discourse for the educated, while Arabic is the common language spoken by semi-educated or uneducated people. This made public reaction to me complex, and I was frequently taken for an Egyptian or Syrian woman. People heard my colloquial eastern dialect of Arabic as classical Arabic, which gave me praise far beyond my ability. I came to understand that the current Islamic revival sweeping Tunisia and other parts of the Maghrib has much to with the restoration of the Arabic language as well as the recovery of Islamic traditions.

The girls, already addicted to American malls, rediscovered the pleasures of the original indoor shopping mall, the Middle Eastern bazaar or *suq*. The jewelry, perfumes, inlaid boxes, leather handbags and Tunisian specialties, such as olive wood carved items or ceramic tiles were a constant source of delight and diversion. They remained shy about the bargaining essential to every purchase, but did not hesitate to enlist my efforts when spending *their* money. A favorite game to play with the eager merchants, especially during the slower winter months, was to have them try to guess our national identity. They would begin with French, and the girls would respond in either French or Arabic, then "Deutsch?"; "Nein", they would reply. "Spanish?", "No, Señor". The last guess, typically, would be English, meaning from England? "Yes, for the language". "You are American?" "American, Bush, America?" (the year was 1990). "Yes, Yes", which was returned with broad smiles, and not a hint of anti-Americanism, only genuine curiosity, and the omni-present greeting, "Marhaba" (Welcome!).

This was at the time of the build-up to the Gulf war when several hundred thousand American troops had been deployed to the Arabian peninsula and we were in the city where the Palestine Liberation Organization has its international headquarters, and where there is tremendous public sympathy for the Palestinians, with a strong anti-war sentiment. Yet we, as an American family, were not subjected to a single unkind word. I could not help but reflect upon this as Arabs and Muslims across the United States became targets for harassment during the several months of the Gulf war.

Where there is ignorance, we seem to fill this void with simple stereotyping, rather than corrective knowledge. We have so little experience with Islam or Muslims in the U.S. that we typically are not even aware of the important holidays, the "'id" at the end of the month of fasting, Ramaḍān, and the "'id" commemorating Abraham's sacrifice of an animal instead of his son, a tradition sacred to all of the Abrahamic faiths, including Judaism, Christianity, and Islam. We hear little of the Hajj, the pilgrimage to Mecca, unless there is a disaster, or some political unrest, as in the heyday of the Iranian revolution. When political reporting by western media people takes place, it frequently is filmed with the correspondent standing in front of a mosque, and is better if the call to prayer can be heard in the background. This lends an air of authenticity, it is no doubt believed, but it also sends a subliminal message that politics, (often of a violent nature, since that is what gets the attention of the media) is associated with the mosque and Islam.

Since the Iranian Islamic revolution and the taking of American hostages in Teheran, and later in Beirut by various extremist religious sects, we have come to fear the religion of Islam. This is a faith practiced by some one billion people in geographical regions extending from West Africa, through North Africa and the Middle East, to India, Pakistan, central Asia, Malaysia and Indonesia. And Islam is projected to be the second most practiced religion in the United States after the millennium. Isn't it time we replace ignorance and stereotyping with knowledge and acquaintanceship? To incorporate a world view shared by Muslims should not threaten our own, nor does knowledge and information mean conversion or blurring of difference. It does mean a newfound appreciation and tolerance that could begin to heal the rifts that have afflicted relations between the West and Islamic societies since their earliest encounters. Certainly in preparation for life in the twenty-first century we can begin to reassess prejudice that is as ancient as the Crusades and as modern as the Islamic revival and begin to redefine the Muslim "other" as fellow human rather than as enemy.

2

The Five Pillars of Islam as Observed by Muslims

The religion of Islam was the last of the great prophetic traditions to emerge from the Middle East, and the revelations made to the Prophet Muhammad are seen as continuous from the time of Abraham, through Moses, to Jesus Christ. Each of the previous prophets is recognized and revered by the religion of Islam.

Islam means "submission," submission to God (Allah), the one and only deity in the uncompromising monotheistic faith. The person who submits is known as a Muslim, although the English transliteration of this term has historically been "Moslem." "Mohammedan" is definitely archaic, erroneous, and offensive, as explained in chapter 1.

The special inner and personal peace that comes to a Muslim who has submitted to God is known as *salaam* and is reflected in the greeting between Muslims, *Essalaam alay kum*. The beauty and simplicity of this greeting is such that it conveys greeting to the individual addressed, while the use of the plural *kum* extends the greeting to all of your kin and beloved, as well as the entire world community of believers. "*Essalaam alay kum*" is an Arabic greeting that is used throughout the Muslim world, irrespective of local language, and is a universal expression among Muslims. When I first learned Arabic in the context of Sudanese and, later, Egyptian society, *Essalaam alay kum* was a greeting used more commonly by men, or by women in more formal contexts. However, with the revival of Islam, the greeting is heard more frequently in public and private as the usual way of saying hello or opening a conversation.

The religion of Islam is rooted in the spiritual and cultural traditions of the Arabian Peninsula. The time of ignorance, the period before the introduction of Islam, is known as the Jāhiliyya, after which came revelation from God of the new religion, reason, enlightenment, and reform. The reference to a time of Jāhiliyya resonates in today's world, as many inspired by contemporary Islamic revival see the dominance of secular ideology or Western culture as another kind of jāhiliyya; thus they see the triumph of an Islamist approach as one which can stem the tide or prevent the return of darkness and ignorance that characterized society before the coming of Islam.

The Muslim calendar begins with the date of the flight, the *Hijra*, from Mecca to Medina in 622 C.E. (common era), when the Muslim community sought refuge and security and was able to expand beyond the small group of followers at Mecca. Underscoring the fact that Muhammad is not conceived of as a divine person, the date of his birth does not begin the Islamic calendar, as Christ's birth begins the Christian calendar. The appropriateness of flight from danger or tactical withdrawal is thus viewed as entirely legitimate from the standpoint of the protection of the Umma. The Islamic calendar follows a lunar cycle, based upon lunar months. Thus there is not a simple 622-year difference between the Muslim lunar and the Western Gregorian solar. For example, 1991–92 A.D. (*anno Domini*) is 1411–12 A.H. (*anno Hegirae*), making a difference of 580 years. To complicate matters a bit more, the Persian-Iranian tradition follows a solar Muslim calendar, making 1992 A.D. the year 1370 A.H., while the Sunni who comprise 90% of all Muslims recognize the date as 1411–12 A.H on the lunar calendar.

The months of the Muslim calendar reflect the annual observance of the faith, such as the month of Ramaḍān, (known as *Farvadin* in the Persian language), or the period following Ramaḍān known as *Dhu al-Hijjah* when pilgrims make the hajj, or the month of *Muharram* when the important 'Id al-Adha (Feast of Sacrifice) takes place. However when we learned Arabic in a decidedly more secular Sudan in 1970, we learned the months as *Shahr Wahid*, "the first month" (January), *Shahr Itnain,* "the second month" (February), and so forth. Today, in the context of revived Islam, the Muslim names of the months are being used again in print and in daily conversation, and one diagnostic feature of an Islamist publication is the use of the Muslim calendar month and year, alone or together with the Western version.

Sources of the Faith, Foundations of the Community

The Holy Book, the Qur'ān, the revealed word of God, is the most fundamental source of the Islamic faith. Its texts, revealed between 610 and 632 C.E. expound matters of belief and practice for individual Muslims, and for Islamic society as a collective, the Umma. The world community of Muslim believers, approaching one billion human beings from diverse cultures, belong to the one great whole, the Islamic Umma.

After the Qur'ān is the *Sunna* of the Prophet, understood as the words and the practice of Muḥammad during his lifetime. The belief that the Messenger was inspired by God established the basis that his life and teachings could be a source of the religion (Esposito 1988:81). The preserved traditions of the Prophet are known as Ḥadīth and constitute the recorded and accepted Sunna of God's Messenger. These fundamental sources of Islam are authoritative and immutable, although they are subject to study and interpretation, as has been the case over the fourteen centuries of the faith. The ones who study and interpret the holy sources are known by various names, such as *'ālim* (sing. "learned one") or *'Ulamā'* (pl.); *mujtahīd* ("one who interprets"); and *feki* or *faqin*, (pl. *foqahā*, "one(s) knowledgeable in *al-Fiqh*, the religious laws"). The common reference to the religious scholars in Western literature on Islam is *'Ulamā'*, so I have used this general term throughout this book, except in specific cultural circumstances where another term is preferred.

The formal interpretation of the holy sources has occurred with the development of Islamic theology, jurisprudence, and law. Islamic jurisprudence (al-Fiqh) has interpreted the sources and devised laws of Muslim religious practice and social behavior that apply to all Muslims, laws which are enforced in Islamic courts by Muslim judges known as *qadis*. Four schools of legal interpretation have developed in the Sunni Muslim tradition, the *Hanafi*, *Māliki*, *Shafi'i*, and *Hanbalī* schools. However, they do not differ significantly with respect to the sources, and their differences are neither doctrinal nor dogmatic.

The Arabic word for "correct path" or "right road" is Sharī'a and this has become the referent for the religious law, since following God's law guarantees that a Muslim will adhere to the straight path and enter paradise after the Final Judgment. Legal theory and social practice of the Sharī'a are discussed more extensively in chapter 6.

Difference Between Sunni and Shī'a Islam

The religion of Islam is divided into two great branches, the Sunni and the Shī'a, with the former branch constituting over 90 percent of the

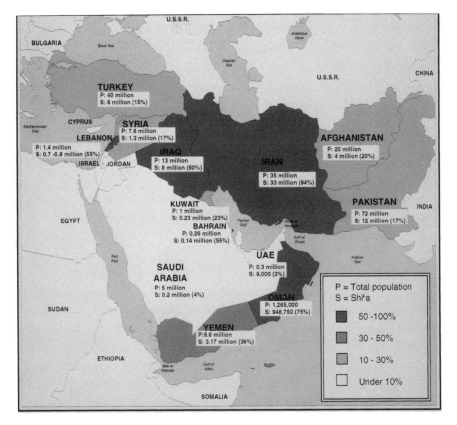

Fig. 2. Shi'ite population in the Middle East. Copyright by Diederik
Vandewalle. Reprinted by permission.

world community of believers. Shī'a Islam, from its origin in the first century of the religion, has been a minority movement within the greater religious community. Unlike the great divide created in Christianity by the Protestant Reformation, and unlike the differences between Orthodox and Reform Judaism, the split between Sunni and Shī'a Islam has more to do with succession, governance, and leadership of the community of Muslims than with differences in theology.

When the Prophet died in 632 C.E., he had appointed no successor, thus leaving to the early Muslim community the decision as to who would be the rightful successor and deputy of God on earth, the khalīfa (caliph). The first caliphate fell to the close companion of Muḥammad, Abū Bakr, and then to two other companions, 'Umar I and 'Uthmān ibn 'Affan during the first twenty-four years of succession after the Prophet. This was a golden period consisting of rule by men who had known Muḥammad, and they are regarded as the Rightly Guided Caliphs from whom inspiration is still derived.

At the time of the accession of the fourth caliph, 'Alī, in 656 C.E., the matter of the rightful succession of caliphs came into question. 'Alī was a cousin and son-in-law of the Prophet, who had married Fātima, the daughter of Muḥammad and Khadījah, who bore him two sons, Hasan and Ḥusayn. With the appointment of a member of the family of the Prophet as caliph, the whole matter of genealogical and dynastic succession was raised. This disagreement led to warfare between Muslims, with supporters of the families of the Prophet and first three caliphs against 'Alī, his sons, and his partisans, known as Shī'at 'Alī. Five years later, in 661 C.E., Mu'āwiyah I laid claim to the caliphate establishing the Umayyad dynasty in Damascus, and in the next year 'Alī was assassinated by former followers disappointed that he had failed to prevent Mu'āwiyah's succession. The Islamic caliphate shifted geographically from the more isolated Arabian Peninsula to Syria, closer to the center of world events, and the subsequent spread of Islam was remarkable and dramatic.

However, when Mu'āwiyah's son, Yazīd I, succeeded his father in 680 C.E., the anger of 'Alī's son could not be contained, and Ḥusayn mounted a rebellion in Kufa, Iraq. His relatively small band of followers was easily defeated and Ḥusayn was murdered at Karbala, Iraq. This martyrdom of both 'Alī and Ḥusayn, from the perspective of the Shiites, represents a historical tragedy and injustice that influences their distinctive view of religious leadership and governance. Many special Shī'a rites commemorate the murders of 'Alī and Ḥusayn, and some of these rites are quite passionate and emotional. The places where the historical battles occurred are sacred places of special pilgrimage.

The Sunni majority and Shī'a minority branches of Islam disagree over the legitimate method of succession to khalīfa, whether by a method of selection or election as in Sunni principle, or by divine succession to Imām through the family of the Prophet. The former view won out in the first century of Islam, and the Shī'a faction has remained a relatively isolated minority living primarily in Iran and Iraq, but with a significant and active population in Lebanon.

During the first century of Islam not only was this difference of politics and succession resolved, but also Islam dramatically spread throughout the Middle East and North Africa into Spain, where Muslim rule dominated the Iberian Peninsula until the expulsion of the Moors in 1492. Islamic religious law, the Sharī'a, was also developed in the first century of Islam in four main schools of Islamic jurisprudence. With the caliphate in place and basic institutions established, Islamic society developed and began to assume a position on the world's stage where it became a force with which Western society would reckon.

The Five Pillars in Practice

The five pillars of the Islamic faith represent its most basic beliefs and practices. Formally, they are derived from the same immutable sources of the religion. To the degree that they vary in expression from one Muslim community to another, they show the influence of the cultural and historical variation within the Islamic Umma. Variations along folk religious lines are often the result of syncretic blends with preexisiting religious trends, but they usually coexist and rarely violate the unchangeable tenets of the faith.

The Shahāda (Testament of Belief)

The first of these, the *Shahāda*, or testimony of belief, asserts the uncompromising monotheism of Islam, continuing the tradition of monotheism begun by Judaism and continued with Christianity. Its most basic concept is the oneness and unity of Allah, tawhīd, is set forth in the first part of the testament, *La Ilallāh,* (There is no deity but Allah). The second part of the Shahāda relates to the Prophet of Islam: *Wa Muhammadun*

Rassoul Allah, (And Muḥammad is His Messenger). Muḥammad as the Messenger of God is the one to whom the Holy Book, the Qur'ān, was revealed, and thus the Prophet Muḥammad exists in the realm of humanity, not of the divine, and is therefore distinguished from Christ, who is believed by Christians to be divine.

The Shahāda, ideally, is the first thing that a child should hear and the last that a dying person should hear. Parents may begin to teach their children how to speak by repeating the Shahāda in the earliest years of life as they are held and nurtured. Pressing the child close, a father may utter "Allahu Akbar (God is all Great). *Ashadu anu la Allah ila Allah* (There is no deity but Allah)."

Our own children, who were beginning to learn articulate speech in the Sudan and Egypt, respectively, learned the Shahāda by continuously hearing the call to prayer and watching the people around them respond by initiating prayer. The Shahāda is recalled with each of the five daily calls to prayer and is an ever-present reminder of the unity and oneness of God.

The invocation of the name of God, "bismiAllah," is an excellent way to begin things and can be heard in everyday speech from the start of meals, to the opening of a class lecture, to starting of a car or the take-off of an airliner. Likewise, the expression *"Inshā 'Allāh"* (God willing) is heard thousands of times daily in hundreds of different contexts, ranging from interpersonal greetings, to the making of appointments, to discussions of politics. The determining of one's fate or condition by God is discussed more fully in chapter 3, but suffice it to say, the name of God is called upon or invoked repeatedly in everyday conversation and is a signature of the use of the Arabic language.

On the side of folk Islam (which is discussed more fully later in this chapter), there has been a certain tendency to revere local holy men, called *sheikhs* or *faqīs* in eastern North Africa and the Middle East and *marabouts* in northwest Africa. Such holy men are said to possess much *baraka* (God's blessings) and in some cases to be able to perform miracles or bring about cures. Frequently, tombs erected at the burial site of such holy men become the objects of worship, veneration, and even pilgrimage, a tendency contrary to tawḥīd and the unwavering monotheism of Islam. Official Islam frowns on such veneration, but these tombs of holy men are very popular with the masses in their everyday religious practice and are especially invoked at times of crisis. However, this practice falls well short of saint worship in Christianity.

New mosque of modern design in Omduran, Sudan.

Salāt (Prayer)

Prayer in Islam repeats the basic elements of the testimony of belief and is recited or, more properly, chanted in the call to prayer by the muezzin who stands atop the minaret of the local mosque and calls the faithful to prayer five times daily. *"Allahu Akbar, Allahu Akbar"* begins the call. *"Ashadu ann la Allah ila Allah* (I witness that there is no God but Allah). *Ashadu anu Muhammadun Rassoul Allah,* (I witness that Muhammad is His Messenger)."

Prayer belongs to the religious realm of *Ibadāt*, personal obligations of Muslims. Before approaching the holy act of prayer the Muslim will perform ritual cleansing by washing the hands and feet, rinsing the mouth and ears. Outside the mosque are fountains and running water for this purpose. Prayer is performed respectfully without shoes, facing in the direction of Mecca (not always to the east, depending upon the geographical location of the Muslim), bowing with the hands at the knees, bowing and prostrating oneself, with the forehead touching the ground. The prayer consists of two to four prostrations depending upon the time of day. Prayer can be performed anywhere, and small prayer rugs can be used for the purpose, stored in a special place or carried with the traveler.

The words of the Muslim prayer repeat the Shahāda, reflect upon the revelation of the Qur'ān, and emphasize the glory and oneness of God. At the end of prayer, the Muslim looks to the left and to the right in symbolic greeting of the Umma, the world community of Muslims.

Typically, no dwelling or place of work is far from a mosque, and in many of the more densely populated neighborhoods where I have lived with my family, there were several mosques within audible distance for the call to prayer. Thus the call often has the effect of surrounding you, enveloping you, reminding you of the time of day, or even awakening you at dawn. There are five prescribed times for the call: at daybreak, noon, mid-afternoon, sunset, and evening. A few zealous Muslims respond to each of the five daily calls to prayer, but for most the demands of daily living make this impractical. Women, who are not salaried employees outside of the home, will usually pray at home perhaps at sunrise and in the evening. Religious men may stop by the local mosque on the way to or from work, but often they pray at dawn and in the evenings, like their wives. Prayer in the mosque is not a necessity, as the Muslim approaches God directly without any need of an intermediary person or place. Women in many Muslim societies do not pray regularly in the mosque; if they do there are separate areas provided for them, since males and females praying together is considered a distraction from the intended singular focus on God.

Communal prayer in the mosque, however, is considered a higher form of prayer because it is collective and involves the broader Islamic community. Friday prayer is congregational and is led by an imām who faces the *mihrāb,* a niche in the architecture of the mosque indicating the direction (qibla) *of Mecca.* The Arabic word for group, *jamā'a,* literally means "to gather," and it is used in reference to the mosque (jāmi'); it is also the root from which the word to describe a university (jāmi'a) is derived, since the earliest universities were religious and were attached to great mosques. Thus the famous Jāmi'at al-Azhar in Cairo refers both to Al-Azhar University and Al-Azhar Mosque, adjacent buildings but with separate identities. Likewise, Jāmi'at Zeitouna in Tunis refers both to the famous Zeitouna Mosque and to the historic university of religious studies before its closing by the secularist leader Habīb Bourgība.

Friday prayers are the largest gatherings of the practicing Muslims and are often led by the imām of the mosque and accompanied by a sermon that focuses on religious, social, or political subjects. In these days of increased Islamic consciousness, attendance at Friday prayers is impressive, with overflow crowds quite typical. Accommodation for the faithful to pray in the courtyard or even in the streets surrounding the mosque is not uncommon, with mats or rugs placed on the ground for this purpose. Collective prayer is performed in unison and is a powerful expression of solidarity with one's fellow Muslims. For some people in the West, who may not understand this or who may have been influenced by anti-Muslim sentiments, this practice appears to be the unthinking performance of fanatics and radicals, adherents of a faith that promotes terrorism. As mentioned above, journalistic reporting of recent events in the Middle East has tended to reinforce this impression by the media use of the mosque-Muslim prayer motif.

Increasingly, with the gathering strength of Islamist forces, the sermon at the Friday service has taken on more overtly political issues, and it may end in exhortations to political action, with demonstrations following the weekly ritual. This was certainly the case during the height of the Islamic revolution in Iran, and postprayer demonstrations are currently a part of Palestinian Islamic resistance to Israeli rule in the occupied territories. In predominantly secular countries currently experiencing Islamic revival, such as Egypt and Tunisia, Friday prayer has taken on a role associated with democratic opposition or Islamist agitation. Some of the central downtown mosques may be under government surveillance, and overt expressions of government force, such as the presence of police or army troops, may be a regular part of Friday prayer. This is not a militarist extension of the Islamic faith, but an expression of the secular government's fear of politicized Islam.

In these days of a generalized Islamic awakening and revival, the call to prayer has taken on heightened symbolic meaning. For example, many of the Islamist groups use the name "The Call" (Da'wa) for their organizations and publications. Furthermore, responding to public pressure from Islamist sympathizers, the call to prayer is often broadcast interrupting daily radio and television programming, even in a highly secularized nation such as Tunisia. The evening broadcast of the call to prayer (al-maghrib prayers) is special because most family members are at home. On television, pictures of the holy places of Mecca and Medina, the Ka'ba, or a famous sheikh chanting the call to prayer may be shown as part of the inspirational moment, the traditional pause that signals the end of the daytime and beginning of the evening's activities. In many of the Arab-Muslim countries, where climates range from temperate to very hot, evening is the time when life begins again after the intense heat of the afternoon. The evening prayers mark the customary transition.

Ṣawm (Fasting During the Month of Ramaḍān)

Although the observance of the religion of Islam is intensely personal and individual, its rituals are highly public and collective. The observance of the annual fast during the month of Ramaḍān, the ninth month of the Islamic calendar, is at once individual and highly social. In the Islamic calendrical system of time reckoning, the Ramaḍān fast moves forward ten days each year. The month of fasting commemorates and celebrates the revelation of the Qur'an by God to Muḥammad.

Fasting for an entire month is a test and personal trial for Muslims and is viewed as a form of personal *jihād* ("struggle"), part of the more difficult inner struggles with the flesh and worldly appetites. Averring food and drink from sunrise to sunset for one lunar month is obligatory for adult Muslim men and women, with only the young, the infirm, pregnant women, and travelers exempted. One mark of the maturing adolescent is the decision to begin to fast, the timing of which is a matter of personal choice.

Fasting is always a struggle, but when the month of fasting falls during the hot summer months, it is especially challenging. Some zealous Muslims observe a devout form of fasting, refusing even to swallow their own spittle; others may add extra days of fasting. Travelers, among the exempted during the days of their journey, are expected to make up the days missed, but this is strictly a matter of personal religious observance.

Those observing the Ramaḍān fast usually rise well before the sun, prepare a light meal (in Egypt and the Sudan this typically consists of seasoned beans with bread and sweet tea), and begin their day with the morning prayer. They refrain from consuming anything by mouth, including cigarettes and chewing gum, throughout the day until sunset, which is usually between 5:00 and 6:00 P.M. By the time of the setting sun, food has been prepared and the family gathers for the Ramaḍān breakfast. In Khartoum traditionally a cannon was fired at this time, with the sound reverberating throughout the whole of the metropolitan area. Nowadays people rely on the radio and television for announcing the time of the day's passing so that the fast can be broken.

Ramaḍān is a time of trial and sacrifice, but it is also a time of celebration and reunion with family, friends, and neighbors. Some of the Ramaḍān greetings and customs are illustrative. Although a time of denial, a typical greeting, "Ramaḍān Karim," translates as "Ramaḍān is abundant (or generous)." Although it is a time of fasting, it is also an occasion for feasting, and special foods are prepared for the nightly guests. The lavishness of such breakfasts varies considerably by class. Wealthier families may entertain large gatherings of business associates and their families, who use the occasion to display their latest fashions and jewelry. Such conspicuous displays of consumption are contrary to the intended simplicity and reflection associated with the fast, and their "waste and inefficiency" were used as a justification by Habīb Bourgība of Tunisia when he recommended the end of fasting during Ramaḍān. However, his controversial suggestion was never implemented because of the multiple religious and social functions that fasting during Ramaḍān represents for Muslims.

While some breakfasts are more elaborate than others, all are characterized by a spirit of generosity, and a simple workman breaking his fast on the street with a meal of bread and beans might invite passersby to join in his Ramaḍān breakfast meal, as has happened to us on numerous occasions. At least one Ramaḍān invitation and reciprocal invite is expected from neighbors and from work and business associates, although multiple family invitations are the norm.

The typical middle-class breakfast is more elaborate than the ordinary main meal, and it may include many special foods, such as a drink made from apricot paste called Mish Mish that is popular in Syria, Egypt, and the Sudan. Meat dishes of kebab, kofta, and vegetarian falafel are popular, as are sweetened macaroni dishes. A special drink made from dried sorghum, called *abrey*, is served especially during Ramaḍān in the Sudan and Egyptian Nubia. Sweet sesame candies, *helawa* made from sesame paste, and other sweets are sold especially during Ramaḍān, and they are offered after the main meal with Arabic coffee or sweetened mint tea. Tunisians prepare a sweet custard made from durra or sorghum, which is served with nuts. In short, all of the best and most highly prized foods are served during Ramaḍān, more from the fact that guests are usually a part of the meal than to satisfy ravenous appetites.

Those who are fasting often describe the first week of the fast as the most difficult physically. However, after the first week many Muslims describe a spiritual peace and sense of balance and contentment derived from succeeding in the internal jihād, and from being part of a vast collective ritual that unites the world's Muslims. This euphoria seems to carry most people right through to the end of the fast, although some are naturally quite tired and even irritable toward the end of Ramaḍān. Businesses, government bureaucracies, shops, and services all slow down and become less efficient because workers have come to the job with perhaps only three or four hours of sleep, having had guests late into the night and awakening before dawn. Western businesspersons and diplomats with long experience in the region have learned to expect that appointments may not be on time during Ramaḍān.

Today, with the increased vitality of Islamic practice, the degree of stigma on public eating has intensified, even to the point of formal bans. In fact the power of this stigma is an excellent measure of the new influence of Islamist movements. In Tunisia, which underwent the most dramatic revisions of Islamic institutions in the Arab world after its independence in 1956, fasting is still viewed as a matter of personal conscience, and some eating establishments are open for business during the fast between sunrise and sunset. A growing Islamist movement in Tunisia condemns this public insult to the majority Muslim community, but so far there has been no militant action to close these restaurants.

When we first lived in Khartoum during the early 1970s, the Ramaḍān fast was viewed as a matter of personal practice that most Muslims performed, but those who declined were not stigmatized. Because one-third of Sudan's population is non-Muslim southerners, many of whom live and work in northern Muslim areas, at that time it was considered a courtesy to them and to others not fasting for some restaurants to remain open. Many of our friends at the University of Khartoum did not fast, and the university's Staff Club was open for lunch as much to serve the Sudanese faculty and staff as to feed the non-Muslim, foreign staff. An associate with a guilty conscience might ask my husband and me to bring back a beverage when we went to refresh ourselves during the hot days, but little was made of this quiet conspiracy. Some foreigners and non-Muslims we knew also fasted during Ramaḍān, and we refrained from eating or drinking in the presence of friends we knew were fasting out of courtesy and as a sign of respect.

With Islamic resurgence in Egypt and the Sudan has come social and political pressure to conform to the standard of performing the fast. When we lived in Egypt during the mid-1980s, increasing numbers of public eating places were closed during the fasting hours, opening only in the evening. Complaints were raised by Coptic Christians who owned certain centrally located eateries, but apart from the five-star hotels and restaurants frequented by tourists, it was difficult to find places to eat in downtown Cairo between sunrise and sunset. Under the Islamist regime in power in the Sudan since 1989, any public eating during Ramaḍān is banned and strictly enforced.

For Sunni Muslims, authoritative word regarding the beginning and the end of Ramaḍān comes from Saudi Arabia, where the religious sheikhs make this determination. When the end of Ramaḍān is announced the great ʿId al-Fitr (Feast of the Breaking of the Fast) begins a three- or four-day celebration, one of the largest and most joyous of the Muslim holidays. New clothes are sewn or purchased for children, streets are decorated with bright lights, and children in Egypt carry lanterns as they go about the streets wishing people "Happy ʾId!" Adults greet each other with similar expressions of good wishes, "ʿId Saʿeed (Happy Holidays)" or "Sana Jadida Saʿeeda (Happy New Year)."

Traditionally, a sheep or goat purchased by the family and slaughtered for the holiday; however, with rising inflation and the increased cost of living, the purchase of an entire animal has become prohibitively expensive for many middle-class families. They may settle for a portion of meat from the butcher or share with the extended family in the purchase of an animal for slaughter. The killing of the animal must be carried out by a skilled Muslim butcher, who cuts the animal's throat and allows it to bleed to death in the prescribed Islamic fashion. The animal is then butchered by the same specialist, who performs the service for a fee or for a portion of the meat. Other portions of the meat are set aside as gifts for family, neighbors, and the poor as a traditional form of charitable behavior. We were frequent recipients of such gifts of meat in honor of the ʿId al-Fitr, and the more we received, the more we were able to engage in the honor of sharing, often ending up at the central mosque downtown, where the poor gather in anticipation of such gifts.

The ʿId al-Fitr is one of the national holidays in predominantly Muslim countries during which intense socializing and celebration take place. It is probably the closest thing socially to the Christmas holiday in the West, although its religious meaning is unrelated and the materialism we have come to associate with Christmas is lacking. But socially it is a time of great coming together and marks the culmination of one of Islam's great annual collective rituals.

The birth of the Prophet Muḥammad, the *Mawlid el-Nabi*, is celebrated but not as a centerpiece of the Islamic faith. It may or may not be a national holiday, and although it is commemorated with reverence, it does not have the same significance as the birth of the Christ does for Christians, because Muḥammad is not held as divine. In Egypt sweet sugar dolls are sold for the Mawlid, whereas the Tunisians prepare a special Mawlid pudding of sweetened sorghum, which is shared with relatives and neighbors.

After the end of 'Id al-Fitr, life returns to its normal routine, unless it is interrupted by a member of one's family who is preparing to make the pilgrimage to the holy places (the *Hajj*) in the recommended time after Ramaḍān.

Zakāt (Obligatory Almsgiving)

Zakāt is the religious responsibility of every Muslim to share with Muslims in need, such as the poor, orphans, or widows, through charitable offerings made both as a matter of personal conscience and as duty. Zakāt as an alms tax has been mandated in government law in certain Islamic republics, and has become a reliable index of successful Islamist politization.

Zakāt is worship of God, as well as an act of thanksgiving and service to the community (Esposito 1988: 92). As a religious tax (usually about 2–3 percent) on one's accumulated wealth or assets, it is not comparable to secular notions of an income tax. It is predicated upon the recognition of the injustice of economic inequity and the responsibility of Muslims everywhere to assist one another and the faith in a material way. Clearly the issue of economic inequality between the oil-rich and poorer Arab-Muslim nations has some political potential. In the past Zakāt was collected and redistributed by the government, but was abandoned as a governmental practice for many centuries. In this current period of Islamic revival the issue of Zakāt has been raised by Islamists as a legitimate activity for a Muslim government to pursue. Pious Muslims have historically performed Zakāt irrespective of the state's official position.

Zakāt in practice can be as simple as giving money to the homeless or sharing meat during the holidays with the poor or with neighbors who are known to be in need. Zakāt offerings are most frequent at the times of the great Muslim holidays, but the poor can be found throughout the year near to the central mosques of major cities where charitable offerings can be made at any time.

Zakāt embraces not only the immediate community in the present time, but it also extends to the larger Muslim society for time immemorial. Certain charitable gifts can be made in the form of bequests offered in the name of God; such a bequest is known as a *waqf* (pl. *awqāf*). Awqāf constitute a special category of Muslim giving and have been administered separately by Islamic states over the centuries, as well as recorded and regulated by agents of secular governments, such as the Minister of Awqāf of the Ottoman Empire. In addition, awqāf have been subject to interpretation and regulation by the Islamic courts. For example, jurists in the twentieth century have ruled that individual bequests of waqf cannot be used to disinherit heirs prescribed by Islamic law.

The idea of this particular form of Zakāt is that it is a gift, made in the name of God, to be held in perpetuity. Awqāf can be bequests of land, or funds to establish or maintain mosques, hospitals, and religious schools. Anything that supports or acts on behalf of the Muslim community can be nominated as a waqf. Substantial gifts of property or sums of money have been subject to regulation, since awqāf cannot be sold or transferred as private property, except according to the original intent of the donor.

Under the influence of the Islamic revival, countries such as Iran, Pakistan, and the Sudan have formally instituted payment of Zakāt by legislative mandate. However, enforcement is problematical since Zakāt has been thought of as a personal duty and not as a matter of state imposition for many centuries before the current wave of Islamist activity. Karām, generosity (which is discussed in chapter 3), is a basic Arab and Islamic value that is fostered in many ways in Muslim society, and a sense of a responsibility to share is certainly reinforced by the Islamic precept of Zakāt.

Performance of the Hajj

The pilgrimage to the Muslim holy places of Mecca and Medina is the final religious duty that every Muslim is asked to perform at least once in her or his lifetime. The focus of the pilgrimage is the Ka'ba, the cube-shaped House of God containing the black stone, given to Ibrahim (Abraham) by the angel Gabriel and thus is a symbol of God's covenant with Abraham's son, Ismail, and, by extension, with the Muslim

Pilgrims circling the Ka'ba in performance of the Hajj in the courtyard of the Grand Mosque at Mecca.

community. The Ka'ba was already a place of pilgrimage in pre-Islamic times, and tradition tells that one of the first things Muhammad did, upon triumphantly entering Mecca, was to cleanse the Ka'ba of its poly-theistic idols and restore it to the worship and veneration of the one true God (Esposito 1988: 93).

The pilgrimage follows the Ramadān month of fasting and is held annually between the eighth and thirteenth days of Dhu al-Hijja, the twelfth month of the Muslim lunar calendar. Its first rite is the donning of the *ihram*, a seamless white garment worn by men and a simple white dress and head covering for women. Many men shave their heads; it is essential that men's heads be uncovered. As they don the ihram, the primary invocation of the Hajj (*talbīyah*) is recited ("Here I am, O God at Thy Command! Thou art without associate"), thus reiterating the fundamental unity and oneness of God. They then proceed to the Great Mosque where the Ka'ba is located and circle it seven times (*tawaf*), symbolizing the unity of God and humans and that human activity must have God at its center. When making the circumambulations of the Ka'ba, pilgrims may touch or kiss the black stone, as did the Prophet in his pilgrimages. According to some traditions the black stone is the sole remnant of the original place of worship built by Abraham and Ismail. The stone has no devotional significance and is not an object of worship itself, consistent with the uncompromising monotheism of Islam (Nawwab 1992: 30). During the days of the Hajj pilgrims pray at the place where Abraham, the father of monotheism, stood; they run between Safa and Marwa commemorating Hagar's search for water for her son, Ismail; they stone three pillars symbolizing evil and Satan; they visit the Plain of Arafat, where they stand from noon to sunset in repentance before God and pray for forgiveness for themselves and for all Muslims (Esposito 1988: 94).

On the third day of the Hajj, many pilgrims slaughter a sheep, goat, or other animal to commemorate Abraham's willingness to sacrifice his son to God (a belief shared by Jews, Christians, and Muslims) and to symbolize Islam's basic tenet of submission to God's will. Muslims all over the world share in this joyous and symbolic remembrance by performing their own sacrifice of animals, the 'Id al-Adha (Festival of Sacrifice). Known also as the 'Id al-Kabir (the Great Feast), it is the completion of the Muslim year and the culmination of the celebration that began with the end of Ramaḍān fasting. Again a portion of the meat from the slaughtered animal is set aside for the poor, as a traditional form of charity. The 'Id al-Adha, like the 'Id al-Fitr, is usually a national holiday in predominantly Muslim countries across the globe, and it represents another dimension of the shared religious and cultural ties that bind the Umma together.

Usually pilgrims precede or follow the Hajj, the greater pilgrimage, with the 'umra (the lesser pilgrimage), which takes place only in Mecca and can be performed at any time of the year. The 'umra shares many features of the Hajj, but it venerates the unique, sacred character of Mecca.

Before the age of air transportation, the journey to the Hijaz was undertaken on foot, by caravan, and by sea; the Hajj journey might take months or even years to complete. Pilgrims from West Africa were known to take five to ten years to complete the journey, often settling down for a time to earn some money to continue. The three great caravan routes of the past were gathered and led from Islam's great cities of Cairo, Baghdad, and Istanbul. Pilgrim routes and trade routes were coexistent and this great tradition of journeying reinforced knowledge of the other and contributed to the spread of Islam (Eickelman and Piscatori 1990).

Typically the pilgrimage is performed only once and after the prime of life has passed, so it is not uncommon to hear the terms of address *Hajj* or *Hajja* (masculine and feminine references to those who have made the pilgrimage) in association with older people. The terms are also used in a generic respectful form of address for older persons for example, when passing in a crowded bus or train, you might say "Excuse me, ya Hajj."

Over the centuries the obligation to perform the Hajj has meant that Muslim peoples of widely disparate geographical and cultural backgrounds mingled in the course of the journey and the actual rituals associated with the pilgrimage. The powerful concept of the Umma, the transcultural, transnational community of believers, becomes real and concrete during the Hajj. The elimination of linguistic, cultural, and racial barriers to contact and communication has had a profound effect on many individual Muslims, especially from lands where racism has been a part of their socialization. The personal and political transformation of the African-American Muslim leader Malcolm X is well documented in his autobiography and on film, with the performance of the Hajj as a critical life experience leading to his renunciation of racialist ideas. In an extraordinary deviation from past practice, director Spike Lee was permitted to travel to the holy places to film the parts of the movie *Malcolm X* that had to do with this historic pilgrimage by an American Muslim. After the Hajj, Malcolm X changed his name to el-Hajj (the one who has completed the pilgrimage) Malik el-Shabazz.

Performance of the Hajj has the power to heal as well as to renew the faith of the Muslim. Those who have suffered tremendous personal tragedy, such as the loss of a spouse or the death of a child, who have made the Hajj often return more at peace with their personal sadness. It is common for older people, upon completion of the Hajj, to declare that they are now ready to die. The Hajj can be both a culmination as well as the signal of a new beginning in life. For those who make it only once, it is the spiritual journey of a lifetime.

Others may use the performance of the Hajj opportunistically, such as a secularist politician making the pilgrimage to prove that he is not anti-Islamic or that he has found new meaning and purpose in religion. Ja'afar al-Numayri of the Sudan marked his political shift from secularist socialism to Islamist orientation by undertaking the Hajj. Others, such as the secularist successor to Habīb Bourgība in Tunisia, Zein Abdine Ben Ali, may make the lesser pilgrimage, the 'umra ("visitation"), to signify publicly their continuing commitment to religion.

The pilgrimage season is notorious for delays in air transportation that result from the sheer numbers of travelers en route to Saudi Arabia. It is a logistical problem that has been solved by special chartered flights for the Hajj and special terminals at international airports. To the Westerner, there is a remarkable lack of rancor or public display of anger at the inevitable delays that are part of the Hajj season travel, but the relative peace is attributable both to the point of the journey and to a more general acceptance of one's fate as part of God's plan, a value discussed more fully in chapter 3.

Folk Traditions and Local Practice of Islam

A good Muslim can observe the five pillars and also follow religious practices that are not strictly Islamic, or may even be thought of as un-Islamic. There is an important distinction between orthodox interpretations of Islam and folk beliefs and practices. Islamic states, whether in the great days of empire and the caliphates or in contemporary times, have fostered and utilized the group of religious scholars known as the 'Ulamā. As the official interpreters of the basic sources of the faith, the Qur'ān and Sunna, they have shaped the religious law, Sharī'a, and have held power and given authoritative opinions by virtue of their association with the state. A religious judge (*qadi*) or the state's mufti (literally "one who opens the way," in this case to official interpretation) could issue a *fatwa* giving the official view of the religion and by extension, the state, on any subject. A fatwa was issued in the early Muslim Sudanese state on the permissibility of consuming the new drink, coffee, and a fatwa was issued in Kingdom of Saudi Arabia on the legitimacy of the presence of non-Muslim troops in the holy places during the Gulf War. Given what we know of history and politics, it is not difficult to surmise the positions taken in these fatwas. They have had the force of law with the power of the state behind them, but their impact has been felt largely in the centers of power, in the cities. Rural folk have generally continued their own particular synthesis of Islam and other religious traditions.

Perhaps the most powerful folk traditions associated with the spread of Islam are the mystical orders, the Ṣūfī brotherhoods known as *ṭarīqa* (pl. *ṭuruq*). The Ṣūfī designation derives from the word for wool, *suf*, referring to the type of garment many early Ṣūfīs wore, thus displaying their lack of concern for worldly comforts. These mystical brotherhoods date back to the early centuries of the spread of Islam and originated in Turkey or Iraq from the famous Qādirīyah *ṭarīqa* founded by ʿAbd al-Qādir al-Jīlānī, who died in Baghdad in 1166. Perhaps the best known of the Ṣūfī poets and teachers was Jalāl ad-Dīn ar-Rūmī (known as Mawlānā) who founded the mystical order of the Mawlawīyah ("Mevlevis" in Turkish), known to the West as the Whirling Dervishes. The Mawlawīyah utilized the words and worldview of simple villagers, without using technical theological vocabulary, and thus they made divine truths accessible to those who were not literate or educated in theological Arabic or Persian. The kind of Islam they invoked was considered by the orthodox urban theologians to be "folkish" and "primitive" (Schimmel 1984: 128). Jalāl ad-Dīn ar-Rūmī's place of worship is Konya in central Turkey, where the famous Dervish dancers perform a *dhikr* ("remembrance"), and whirl to bring about an ecstatic religious state and spiritual union with God. From the standpoint of orthodoxy, there is nothing wrong with the veneration of God. But Mawlānā, in his thirteenth-century evangelism for converts to the pursuit of the mystical path to God, called *all* to Konya: "Come, Come, even if ye be an idolater or fire worshipper, Come to Konya!"

Music, dancing, and the exploration and cultivation of the spirit mark the Ṣūfī tradition, which has sprung from the deepest heart and soul of Islam, but has grown at the periphery of the state and has had a sometimes uneasy relationship with official Islam. I recall being warned by a Sharīʿa judge and a member of the Sudanese ʿUlamāʾ in 1979 to stay away from the performances of the Dervish Dance that my husband and I used to frequent on Friday afternoons: "That is not Islam," he would say, "and you are here to study proper Islam."

On the other hand, the appeal of the Ṣūfī orders is magnetic and undeniable, and it is the means by which Islam spread into the rural hinterlands in the early formative centuries of the new faith. The Ṣūfīs' approach is informal and humanistic. Consider the response I received when I queried the direct descendant of Jalāl ad-Dīn ar-Rūmī in Istanbul in 1972 as to why the dervishes whirl in their dhikr.[1] He said that in the days of the Prophet Muḥammad, a new Muslim convert approached the

Prophet and asked him if God was pleased with him. The Messenger of Islam responded by saying that God wanted to know if the convert was pleased with Him. As the story goes, this simple retort produced an ecstatic state in the new convert who began to whirl in joy and happiness.

Although the Ṣūfīs are mystics and ascetics, they are not like members of Christian monastic orders. Sufism does not espouse celibacy, because as the Prophet said, "There is no monkery in Islam" and "Marriage is my way" (Schimmel 1984: 122). Individual Ṣūfīs may travel about, and they figure prominently in local folk and literary traditions referring to the stranger coming to the village from the desert carrying only his staff. However, Ṣūfī orders are based in local areas and find their adherents among local believers.

We often used to attend the dhikr of the Qādirīyah ṭarīqa, held at the tomb of a local holy man, Sheikh Hamad al-Nīl, in Omdurman. We were able to have a taste of rural life and still be close to the city. The performance of the dhikr is by men, but women may attend to receive the blessings of the remembrance of God. While the members of the order are all dressed in white *jellabiyas*, (loose, ankle-length robes), the leader and Dervishes may be dressed in green jellabiyas, or in *jibbas*, a patchwork quilted shirt and pants, signifying disavowal of worldly possessions and recalling the garb of the followers of the Sudanese Mahdī Muḥammad Aḥmad. For about two hours before sunset on Friday afternoons the Dervishes form a circular procession to drum, dance, and sing the praises of God, and the Messenger, Muḥammad. The Dervishes whirl in rapid bursts of energy, which in the heat of the afternoon sun can bring about an ecstatic trance-like state. The dancers are left alone to recover while the others continue the dhikr until sunset, when the ritual stops and the followers depart with the farewell *Essalaam alay kum*.

The tension between folk expressions of Islam, such as the Ṣūfī brotherhoods, and orthodoxy is most apparent in the practice of veneration of local holy men. Revered in life and worshiped after death, they are often regarded as miracle workers and persons from whom one can obtain *baraka* (blessings). Frequently tombs are erected at their burial site, and may become places where dhikrs are held, or they may be sites of local or regional pilgrimage. The marabout tradition in the Maghrib, in northwestern Africa, is part of this folk expression of Islam, and tombs of local holy men dot the North African landscape.

Clearly this veneration of men is contrary to the fundamental principle

Marabout's tomb, object of local veneration, southern Tunisia.

of tawḥīd, the absolute oneness of God, and the veneration of the Prophet of Islam has been greatly curtailed in Islamic practice. Visitation of the burial site and associated mosque of Muḥammad is not mandatory in the performance of the Hajj and may only be added at the beginning or end of the pilgrimage, or it may be performed as a part of the lesser pilgrimage. However, the attraction of these holy men, known as *faqih* or *sheikh*, is more powerful than are the constraints of theological Islam. Rural, perhaps illiterate, people continue to visit the local tombs with supplications for cures, for solutions to problems, or for fulfillment of deep desires. They may bring children to receive blessings from the sheikh, and they may leave small gifts or tie a brightly colored piece of cloth nearby as a token of their visit.

There are other practices commonly found in Muslim societies that belong distinctly to the realm of folk superstition and are not associated with Islam. Perhaps the best known of these are the set of beliefs associated with the evil eye, which are found across a broad spectrum of geography and cultures. Found in Mediterranean Muslim culture as well as in non-Muslim cultures, the evil eye probably can be traced to Pharaonic Egypt and the powerful Eye of Horus. Beliefs surrounding the evil eye emphasize the need for protection, especially for the most vulnerable of humans, infants and small children. Amulets with the familiar bright blue stone with the yellow eye are pinned on children's clothing or hung over cribs; evil eye amulets may be found at the doorways or entrances to Egyptian homes, perhaps alongside beautiful works of Islamic calligraphy. Men may carry evil-eye amulets in their pockets with their car keys or pocket change, while women may wear small pieces of jewelry, rings, or necklaces, with the evil-eye symbol.

It is thought to be a dangerous solicitation of the power of the evil eye to complement a child on his or her beauty or attractiveness, and some rural women may purposefully dress their children in less attractive clothes so as not to attract the attention of the evil eye. Likewise, it is considered imprudent to complement a family too much on its possessions, or to give excessive praise to a woman's jewelry or clothing. Jealousy is thus held in check and humility promoted. Social scientists have suggested that the social control imposed by the limitation on ostentatious displays of wealth explains the continuation of evil-eye beliefs and practices.

Another practice rooted in Islamic traditions but definitely belonging to the arena of superstition is the belief in the power of the written religious word, as found among many Sahelian African Muslims. Writing and literacy are strongly promoted in Islam because of the powerful motive studying and writing the Qur'ān. The traditional Islamic school, the *kuttab* or *khalwa*, focused exclusively on learning to read and write the Qur'ān. Islamic art, with its ban on representational art, has developed an elaborate tradition of religious calligraphy. The calligraphy adorning mosques is a graphic portrayal of the word of Allah. Illiterate Muslims were thus impressed with the writing of God's words which led to the belief that the words themselves can cure or bring about the desired solution to a problem.

A supplicant might visit a local religious man and ask for a recommendation of a Qur'ānic verse to suit his or her problem. The sheikh would write the appropriate verse on a piece of paper and place it in a ḥijāb, a covering made of leather or silver, and the ḥijāb is then worn until the desired end has been achieved, or it may never be removed. Likewise the sheikh may write passages from the Qur'ān or Ḥadīth on a *lawḥ*, a wooden writing board used in Islamic schools, and then wash the ink from the board. The supplicant drinks the inky water with the belief that a solution to the problem will be found.

Within the realm of Islam but inhabiting the domain of the spirit world are the *jinn*, beings that have been part of Middle Eastern folk culture for millennia, and they have even entered Western culture in the form of the "genie" stories. There is a story that when the Messenger of Islam first began to hear the call of the angel Gabriel to recite the words later compiled as the Qur'ān, he was frightened and reluctant, fearful that people would think him possessed or inspired by jinn (Esposito 1988: 9).

Belief in the jinn is widely held, comprising a broadly expressed system of ideas regarding the visitation of spirits, especially at night, and their influence on human activities and endeavors. Jinn visit with the howling winds, or they surprise humans by making appearances in ordinary places in and about the house. They can be simply mischievous, or they can determine the fate of a human, as in the well-known story of the genie and the three wishes. They are a part of the supernatural world, a world that commonly intrudes upon human experience and is troublesome, but a world that is respected and to a degree placated.

A well-documented, but non-Islamic type of supernatural activity is that associated with Zār spirit possession, which is found in the Nile Valley and Ethiopia as well as in Sahelian western Africa, where it is sometimes known as Bori cult. It is a form of spirit possession practiced by Muslims and non-Muslims alike and is the special province of women, who are both the possessed and the exorcists who drive out the spirits causing the illness or depression. Women who are possessed claim that some illness, personal difficulty, or unfulfilled desire is responsible for the spirit possession. Such women host their own Zār parties where a woman *sheikha* presides, animals are slaughtered, and drumming, dancing, and spiritual possession of attendees as well as of the afflicted woman take place. Various spirits appear and possess susceptible women, such as the European or khawāja spirit, or the Ethiopian woman in Nile Valley traditions. My attendance at a Zār party was valued by the other attendees, given the exotic nature of the spirits who visit. After these spirits have spoken, sometimes intelligibly and directly addressing the problem at hand, the possessed woman collapses and some catharsis appears to have taken place. At Zār parties women talk and act in ways otherwise unacceptable in Islamic society, such as smoking or using crude language. Zār has been analyzed as psycho-drama (Kennedy 1967), and more recently as a type of spiritual femi-nism (Boddy 1989). However one interprets it, it operates outside the framework of Islam, although many good Muslim women are fervent believers and practitioners.

Notes

1. I express grateful acknowledgment to the family of Ogüz Bozkurt in Istan-bul, Turkey, for arranging this meeting for me.

3

Islamic Values and Social Practice

Perhaps if the recent history of the world were different and Western society did not have the imperial advantage that it has inherited from the legacy of colonialism and economic domination, we might have studies of our culture by non-western people. A chapter entitled "Western Values and Social Practice" in such a study might include sections on individualism, self-sufficiency, entrepreneurial spirit, male supremacy, or optimism. The treatise, written in Arabic, might be read in translation by some "natives" who think it is reductionist and a simplification of their complex, multifaceted social reality. Others, desiring a basic knowledge of the "other" (i.e., the Westerner), might find the study helpful as an introduction to some of the values underpinning Western society. Turning back to world realities today, the truth is that very little is known or understood about the basic values underlining Muslim society, and in this chapter I offer that kind of basic introduction.

Arab and Muslim

Islam originated in Arabia, the Ḥijāz, in the seventh century of the common era and was founded upon the existing Arab culture there. The Arabs occupied Arabia for at least three millennia before the introduction of Islam; about 1000–500 B.C.E. the camel was domesticated, enabling the Arabs to develop a distinctive way of life dependent upon it for food, drink, clothing, shelter, and transport. The culture these Arabs developed left no great buildings but a rich world view is embodied in their language and poetry.

Of the Bedouin it has been said that their one great monument is their poetry (Polk 1974: vii). It is a poetry sprung from solitude, from privation, from social interdependence and nurtured in the soul of a people. The poems of the ancient Bedouin extol the virtue of generosity and the bravery of the warrior. But the warrior must not be an uncouth barbarian; without diminishing his worth as a warrior, he must strive to be a poet, a man of beautiful and important words. The ancient ode (*qaṣīda*) was composed to be sung; it typically evoked the importance of people and not places, and included praise of one's own people, and of bravery, yet of skill in the verbal arts of rhetoric and argument, as well as of generosity and hospitality among one's companions (Polk 1974: xviii). The art of recitation was practiced by the *rawi,* of which there was at least one in every extended clan, whose task it was to memorize the poetry in order to entertain or educate fellow clansmembers. Such recitations would occur once the camp was settled at night, refreshed in the cool of the evening air. The audience was not passive, but broke in with commentary or recitations of their own, all to savor the art of the poet. Recitations by women and female poets were not uncommon in the pre-Islamic and early Muslim eras.

The images of the camel, the gazelle, the wild ass, and of the desert itself still inspire the contemporary Arab poet, even though she or he may be an urbanite who has never known desert life directly. The powerful similes and metaphors of the poetic tradition have enriched everyday speech and have made Arab compliments all the sweeter and insults all the more devastating.

I have often been struck by the number of men one meets in the Arab world who, despite their chosen profession of law or engineering, or even those with limited education, proclaim as their deepest wish the desire to write poetry. In the same vein, the number of lower and middle class working people Richard and I have met over the years, while traveling long distances on trains or meeting regularly at a café, who proudly declare themselves to be poets is a phenomenon that at first amazed us, but that we came to admire greatly. The power of the word in pre-Islamic Arabia was greatly reinforced by the focus on the revealed word of God to the Prophet Muhammad, the Qur'ān. It remains to this day the highest standard of literary achievement and the most classical form of the Arabic language. The point is stressed in an oft-recited Ḥadīth from the Prophet that the ink of the writer is more precious than the blood of the warrior.

Although the Arabs developed their culture in a desert environment, by the time of the coming of Islam Arabia was well connected to the rest of the ancient world through a complex system of trade routes crisscrossing the Arabian peninsula and flourishing along the coast. Mecca was such an established trade center at the time of the birth of Muhammad in ca. 570 C.E. But desert culture survives in the Arabic language and in many customs associated with Arab culture. The basic greeting in Arabic, "*Ahlan wa Sahlan*" is difficult to translate literally, but means something like "Hello, Be at ease here." The harsh environment of the desert meant that relatively scarce resources, such as water and pasturage, were carefully regulated. Strangers could be violators of such customary rights, but once welcomed, the stranger had no need to fear for his security. "*Ahlan wa Sahlan*" is the secular Arab greeting; "*Es-salaam alay kum*" is the Islamic greeting that is used by both Arabic-speaking Muslims and by non-Arab Muslims as the universal salutation.

Generosity (*Karām*), extolled in the ancient Bedouin poetry, is a core value in Arab society the importance of which has not diminished over the centuries or been fundamentally transformed by urban life and empire, by class division and social stratification. *Karāma* ("honor") is a term that characterizes this sense of generosity and the moral integrity that is conveyed by it; a person who is described as generous is referred to as *karīm* (m.) or *karīma* (f.). Karāma is one of the best of human attributes and is used liberally in discussions of possible marriage mates, in complimentary references to friends, and to describe the good acts of public figures such as politicians. Karāma can be used interchangeably in meaning with dignity; by extension, the selfish person loses her or his personal dignity.

The survival value of generosity within the context of the harsh and unpredictable desert life is obvious; in addition, sharing constructs an intricate web of relationships in the bonding and reciprocity between individuals and groups that has enabled desert families not only to survive, but also to reproduce and flourish in their challenging environment. Where land is not private property and possessions are minimal and portable, sharing of life's necessities is valued. The last draught of water, loaf of bread, or portion of meat is given to the guest over the family member without fanfare on the part of the donor or great expression of appreciation on the part of the recipient. Sharing is so deeply engrained that to notice its expression is an oddity to any but the outsider. Even a passing visitor, without particular need, offends the host if he or she refuses the cup of coffee or tea. For example, Richard and I quickly learned that in response to the question "Won't you have something to drink," "No thanks, I'm not thirsty" is incorrect and socially unacceptable. Even if you have drunk tea or coffee at the offices of a half-dozen bureaucrats before this moment of invitation to drink, you should accept and drink again. To do otherwise implies disinterest in both the traditional hospitality and in the nature of the business you wish to transact.

As Americans we are trained to say "Thank you" for what might be viewed in other cultures as common courtesy or normal human behavior. We thank people for their time, for talking to us or remembering us, for their sympathy; the clerk and the customer thank each other; the parent and the child thank each other for their love. As Richard and I learned Arabic, we made the normal transpositions of English language usage into the new language we were learning. Thus we were thanking people for everything from serving us tea or coffee, to thanking local scholars for the time they had spent with us, to thanking the bus driver, trying in our way to be polite. When people would smile wryly or not respond with the appropriate "You're welcome" to our repeated thanks, we began to see that our sense of gratitude reflected our cultural background, in which generosity is not commonplace and the anonymity of everyday life and exchange is, perhaps, eased by polite but not very meaningful expressions of thanks.

The sincerity of our generosity was tested one early December morning in Khartoum when Muḥammad Aḥmad, the *ghaffir* ("caretaker") of the houseboat on the Blue Nile where we were living, came to our door asking a simple question of my husband. "How many sweaters do you have?" he asked. Since we had learned many Arabic phrases and expressions from Muḥammad Aḥmad, we were pleased to respond correctly, "three sweaters." "Fine," he said, "give me one; winter is coming and I have no sweater." Taken aback, we reviewed the request, commenting to ourselves that he had not even said "Please." To reject his request would be to place our good relationship in jeopardy, we thought, so it was best to offer him a sweater. A few minutes later, when we presented him with a sweater, he took it and did not say "Thank you." At the time we were miffed, but as the months passed Muḥammad Aḥmad brought us many small items from the market, dates, sesame candies, and the like, and we continued to say "Thank you." He would walk away mumbling to himself, "Okay, thank you, thank you," as if to just say the words to please us. Genuine *karāma* is in the deed and not in the words.

Generosity/dignity is one of the ninety-nine qualities of Allah and is referred to in the popular male name 'Abd al-Karim (literally, "slave of God, the Generous"), or in the female name Karima. Generosity has broad social meaning and is recognized as being a quality of the spirit and soul.

Some Westerners are suspicious of this hospitality, especially when it is encountered in a tourist shop and repeated greetings, "Ahlan wa Sahlan" or "Marhaba" ("Welcome!) along with offers of drinks of tea, coffee, or a soft drink are made in an effort to have you, the buyer, extend your stay a little longer in the shop. Staying longer and having something to drink meets the twin goals of extending a welcome and encouraging a closer look at the items for sale. Perhaps this distrust on the part of Westerners stems from the degree of alienation which exists in Western societies, or perhaps it comes from certain negative, preconceived notions about Arabs and Muslims. Whatever its cause, it can result in miscommunication, upset, and a reinforcement of negative stereotypes on both sides. Westerners are often thought of as distant, aloof, and noninteractive. When pressed in a bazaar to "Come in, have a cup of tea, and see my shop," the Western tourist often declines with a certain measure of suspicion about the sincerity of the invitation. The Westerner usually does not understand that he or she could actually sit amicably and sip tea or Pepsi and visit with the storekeeper for nothing more than a pleasant chat without the obligation to buy. The hope is, of course, that you have had a pleasant respite, will return another time, and perhaps even bring a friend to enjoy this hospitality, but there is no specific obligation to do so. All such interactions are played out in an atmosphere of generalized hospitality that may or may not have some specific return.

Given the anonymous nature of buyer-seller interactions in the West, the same tourist is often surprised to find that the shopkeeper both recalls his or her face and the conversation they shared, despite the fact that many days, weeks, or even longer periods of time have passed. This puzzle to the Westerner is readily explained by the close personal relations that pervade every activity, including commerce and trade. Cultural differences and potential misunderstandings between Western and Middle Eastern businesspeople are discussed further in Chapter 5.

The twin values of generosity and hospitality are generalized throughout Arab and Muslim society and straddle class differences, although expressed in different ways. No matter what the class level, it is important to give the appearance of abundance. Preparing more food than can be consumed by guests and encouraging them to eat more and fill themselves beyond normal capacity is customary. Complementing the delicious food and indicating that one is finished by praising God is usually not sufficient to end the meal. Various hosts present at the meal will encourage the guest to continue, often implying that not to continue would be an insult, so that often the guest indulges in a bit more food consumption. Notions of hospitality extend to a social pattern of frequent visits between relatives and friends that often last late into the night, despite work schedules in the morning. The guest may have tried to leave several times, citing the lateness of the hour or commitments the next day, but the host will discourage such leave-taking with remonstrances such as "No, it's still too early." Having been in this situation ourselves many times and feeling a Western sense of frustration about time and logistics of transportation, Richard and I have often been pleasantly surprised to find that our hosts had arranged for and paid for our transportation home, or they would accompany us to a taxi stand and wait until we were safely on our way home.

Displays of generosity that we in the West would find incredulous are an everyday occurrence, so embedded are the values of generosity and hospitality in Islamic life. In addition to numerous free taxi rides because a friendly conversation had ensued, Richard and I received free dental service because "You are a guest in our country." Likewise offers of assistance in the realm of automobile breakdowns and repairs (of which there have been many) added to an appreciation of the depth of these values. Sometimes, when our vehicle had broken down or had a flat tire, other motorists would stop and spend the better part of an afternoon getting the vehicle going again. When we realized that any offer of money as gratitude would be deeply insulting, we had to be creative about finding culturally appropriate ways to express our thanks. We would often obtain the name and address of the person and drop by the house for a visit with a gift of fruit or sweets, never a necessity. Thus new relationships could be formed and continued, and the non-kin network of cooperative relations on both sides was expanded. What did people want from us? They wanted the external network, in the form of information and access to the West.

The contrast between American suspicion of generous acts and Middle

Eastern hospitality is clear in a story related to me by a Sudanese living in the United States. He had stopped by an American roadside to help a stranded female motorist with a flat tire. When he stepped out of his car to approach the woman with an offer of assistance, she rolled up her window, locked the car doors and screamed for help. He tried to explain that he was only there to offer assistance, but to no avail.

Although the poorer members of a family may experience some shame because they cannot provide the same generous hospitality displayed by richer family members, such differences are usually overlooked in public, with the highest value placed on overall family solidarity. In these times of economic difficulty for many in the relatively poor nations of the Arab and Muslim world, it has become a source of shame and disgrace that hospitality cannot be extended in the ways that have been customary in the past. Families may be unable to offer meat as often as they would like to their guests, or they simply will make excuses for not getting together more often. Social visiting beyond the extended family becomes constrained, as it is shameful to invite guests to one's home without providing adequately for them. This is a very contemporary social tension that symbolizes, for the average person, the cultural changes that are occurring as a result of economic hardship.

In the broader realm of social differences between the richer and poorer Muslim nations, much is related about the excesses and waste that can occur when engaging in conspicuous displays of hospitality and generosity. The most prosperous strata of Arab-Muslim society may engage in some notoriously wasteful examples of such consumption, which are witnessed and reported by servants from the poorer nations. For example, a whole sheep may be slaughtered and cooked for two or three guests while the residue is discarded. Such practices have occurred within the context of recent acquisition of unprecedented wealth, and conspicuous consumption in this manner debases the essential qualities of these longstanding cultural patterns.

The Collective in Society and Religion

The idea of the group (*Jamā'a*) in Islamic society is fundamental to the powerful collective consciousness that the religion of Islam promotes. It is expressed in its most all-embracing form in the concept of Umma, the world community of believers, some one billion people from widely differing geographical and cultural backgrounds. Umma derives from jamā'a and connotes unity within the collective. The choice of words for the idea of the United Nations in Arabic opts for the use of *Umam Muttahidah,* rather than the more common term for state or republic, *jamhūriya.* Umma is meant to be a powerful unified collective. It was upon this concept that Julius Nyerere drew in his enunciation of *Ujamaa* as a political and social philosophy to unite Tanzanians in the common purpose of building the new nation-state.

On a more prosaic level, jamā'a can be used to refer to the group of one's friends or classmates, but it also is readily elevated to more significant group activity, such as groups which collect in the mosque. Although the more formal term *masjid* (place of prostration or prayer) may be used to designate a mosque, the term *jāmi'* is the popular, common referent for the local community mosque where group prayer takes place.

From the earliest times of Muslim education, the place of learning—where the Qur'ān and Sunna could be studied in conjunction with writing and reading of Arabic—was the grand mosque, usually centrally located in a large city. These places of learning associated with mosques also became known as *jāmi'as.* Thus the word for university grew out of the word for mosque, which itself indicates group life and gathering for a religious purpose.

The sense of the group and the collective is so entwined with Islam, its rituals, and its society that it is difficult to discuss as a separate subject. I have already emphasized the importance of collective ritual in the discussion of the practice of Islam through the five pillars. In addition, for the most part, the collective rituals are embedded in social practice where the cultural value of the extended family and of group life is already well established. It is difficult for Muslims living in the West to maintain the integrity of the collectivity in their practice of Islam; for example, fasting during Ramaḍān is difficult in a society that neither acknowledges nor appreciates the rites associated with Islam. But many converts to Islam from the West are seeking an attachment to a community and an enlarged sense of group identity when they embrace Islam. Others may be actively rejecting an identity that Western society has placed upon them, as is the case with large numbers of African-Americans who have historically turned to and continue to turn to Islamic alternatives.

The collective and group life are treated more thoroughly in chapter 4, where I examine matters of family, neighborhood, and community.

Honor (Sharāf)

Honor is a fundamental value that is at once highly personal and individual and also utterly collective, rooted in family and group dignity and identity. *Sharāf* is a quality desired in all people. The man's name *Sharīf* identifies an honorable man, and the desirable quality of the bride-to-be is signified by describing her as *sharīfa* (an honorable woman). When guests arrive, the most elegant and formal greeting offered by the host is *"Itsharafna"* (It honors us [that you have come]). The guest might respond, *"Itsharaft ana"* (I am honored).

Sharāf goes much deeper than good manners. Honor embodies the pride and dignity that a family possesses due to its longstanding good reputation in the community for producing upright men and women who behave themselves well, marry well, raise proper children, and above all adhere to the principles and practice of the religion of Islam. A good Muslim family has its honor intact and produces sons who are sharīfs and daughters who are sharīfas.

Honor is understood in a complex way as the absence of shame, for honor and shame are bound to one another as complementary, yet contradictory ideas. *'Ayb* (shame) falls upon a family when a member of the family, especially its more vulnerable female members, conducts herself or himself improperly or gives the appearance of improper conduct. Much of this misconduct is construed as being of a sexual nature. A dishonorable man is one who shirks his familial responsibilities, wastes his money on frivolities or drink, or conducts himself in a way that suggests loose morals. A woman's honor can be placed into question for much less serious conduct or accusation. A woman who goes out alone frequently at night or wears clothing, adornments, or excessive perfume that draw the attention of men can be gossiped about and accused of being dishonorable. In more conservative societies, a woman who has spent time alone with a man classified as a stranger (not a relation) can be accused of dishonor. As such, women respond by dressing modestly and carrying themselves in public society in a restrained way and thus are recognized as above reproach. The double-standard code of conduct, familiar to the West, is discussed more thoroughly in the section of chapter 4 dealing with male-female relations as well as in the discussion of Islamic revival and new forms of protective dress for women.

Shame in the Rearing of Children and the Reproach of Adults

The entwined relationship of honor and shame has been long recognized in both and Arab and Muslim societies as well as in the generalized Mediterranean social complex (Gilmore 1987; Peristiany 1966). 'Ayb (referred to above as the absence of honor, or shame) is a concept that is used liberally in the rearing of children and in the reproach of adults. "'Ayb", whose closest English equivalent is "Shame on you," is usually not applied in the training of very young children, because it implies a degree of prior knowledge and instruction that would have dictated a different course of action. Older children who have disobeyed or have behaved in a disrespectful manner often hear a lecture from a parent or close adult member of the extended family that begins and ends with the admonition "'ayb."

As a collectivist society, it is not uncommon to hear nonrelated adults reprimanding children, usually boys, who are misbehaving or getting into mischief in the streets with the familiar "'Ayb, 'Ayb alay kum" (Shame on all of you). What is most surprising to Western adults is that the boys usually listen to the reproach, modify their behavior, and do not respond with some curse or insult.

The power of the use of the negative value of shame is that it reinforces the positive idea that one's behavior is a direct reflection of one's personal honor and dignity, and that one's personal behavior represents a part of the important whole of family honor. One's sense of honor is acquired in later childhood and remains with the person throughout life.

Adults arguing with each other and trying to make a point often invoke the concept of 'ayb, that somehow the behavior or words in question have brought about a diminution of honor and therefore represent something shameful. Foul language is undignified and shameful; losing one's temper and shouting insults is shameful; failing to come to the aid of a family member or neighbor when one is able is worthy of the reproach "'ayb"; failing to support family members for whom one is responsible is dishonorable and shameful; gossip that potentially causes harm is improper and shameful. Anything that adversely and unfairly affects the dignity of another person is likely to draw the criticism "'*Ayb.*"

In a related vein, conditions of life that do not permit the normal course of events to prevail may also be described using the concept of 'ayb. A broadly accepted ground for the judicial divorce of a woman from her impotent husband is known as *ṭalāq al-'ayb,* in this instance a defect in the man that is shameful. The shame of impotence reveals a great deal about societal views of male dignity and honor. Impotence is legally determined by meeting a set of conditions whereby the couple cohabit in suitable privacy for a prescribed length of time during which the consummation of the marriage can occur; if it does not occur, the wife testifies or the husband admits his impotency and a divorce is granted.

Honor, Shame, and Homicide

Personal and familial honor is such a powerful cultural value that its breach can result in dire consequences, even violence and death. An exchange of insults between men or women sting most deeply when they impugn family or personal honor. They are the fighting words that can make tempers flare and portend an immediate response or deferred rage and revenge. In a study of over four hundred cases of homicide in the Sudan that I conducted for my doctoral research, I found that an insult, often coupled with the threat of sexual jealousy or impropriety, is a major context in which homicide will occur. If the circumstances already mentioned are associated with drinking and inebriation and if weapons are present, the probability that violence and murder will occur increases markedly (Fluehr-Lobban 1976).

Direct insults between husband and wife, such as "You were not a virgin when we married!" or "You are impotent!" are dangerous and harmful. Such insults can lead to violence or can be brought up in court as evidence of shameful and insulting behavior that makes life for the couple intolerable. Insults between men suggesting that their wives or sisters are whores or that their mothers were prostitutes and that they are consequently bastards are so deeply provocative that aggression, violence, or threats must necessarily follow. Insults that curse the religion of the opponent, therefore Islam, are likewise provocative and can occur in the context of violence or can be the direct cause of the violence. These examples suggest that a sense of personal dignity and honor stems from attitudes about good sexual conduct and self esteem derived from religion. Insults impugning a lack of personal generosity or other forms of individualistic behavior are not as likely to result in aggression or violence.

The right of the father and/or brother to punish by death the daughter or sister who has been judged guilty by her kin of sexual misconduct, either by compromising circumstances or public witness and testimony, has been long upheld in Arab society and not specifically rejected by Islamic interpretation. Honor is thereby restored to the family by "washing the shame with blood," and true to the double standard of patriarchal societies, the penalty falls on the accused woman and not on the man with whom she is alleged to have had sexual relations. In some conservative communities, the mere suggestion of impropriety can be met with a physical beating, a clear warning to the woman to avoid more serious entanglements. This traditional customary right has generally not been challenged in the applied law of Muslim societies, although several verses in the Qur'ān would support lesser punishments, such as flogging or house confinement, and forgiveness after repentence [*Sura* ("Verse") 4: 15–18; Sura 24: 1–9].

As in South America, where a similar right of the husband to defend his honor by killing his unfaithful wife remained unchallenged until 1991, it has been left to feminist and political agitators to bring about reform (Morgan 1984: 20). Many feminists from a broad spectrum of Arab and Muslim societies have written and lectured about this problem as an indefensible relic of conservative attitudes towards women (Mernissi 1975; El-Saadawi 1980). Honor, construed as a set of values that confines the ambitions and restricts the mobility of women within a web of fear of possible allegation of sexual misconduct, is in need of modern reinterpretation. Like other social issues discussed in this book, the best method of social reform is initiated from within, by those desiring change with the necessary courage to seek it and achieve it.

Acceptance of One's Personal Destiny or Fate

A great deal has been written and alleged about Arab and Muslim fatalism. More superficial analyses have focused on the invocations, *Inshā' Allāh* (if God wills it), and *Al-Hamdulillāh* (God be praised), by which virtually every action or condition of being is prefaced or concluded.

"I will meet you at 10 o'clock in the morning, *inshā' Allāh*," which usually means that the appointment will be kept, but if my car breaks down or if I am sick which I cannot foresee and only God knows, I will not be able to be there at 10 o'clock. If my car broke down or in spite of feeling ill I managed to keep the appointment, *"Al-Hamdulillah"* (Praise be to God).

There are many jokes among Westerners who have spent long or continuous periods of time in Arab and Muslim society about *"Inshā' Allāh."* These usually refer to the Westerner trying to get something accomplished with a government bureaucrat or small businessman, and the Westerner is told to "Come back tomorrow, everything will be ready, *inshā' Allāh.*" Of course, the Westerner returns the next day and is told, "Really, tomorrow, *inshā' Allāh.*" The sense of frustration and clash of worldviews is evident in a well-known Western parody and renaming of select Arab corporations as I.B.M., for *"Inshā Allāh"* (God willing), *"Bukra"* (Tomorrow), and *"Ma' Lesh"* (Never mind). In the short run tempers have flared, however in the long run patience is a virtue.

Everyday greetings and expressions of interest in the well-being of others are rooted in continual references to the influence of God: "How are you?" "I am well, praise God" or "I am not very well, praise God." Irrespective of one's physical condition, God is the defining force. "And how are your children?" As the conversation progresses with inquiries about family, job, and well-being, it is not necessary to describe the condition of each, but simply to reply "Al-Hamdulillah" to each question. The formula for the opening of conversation between individuals is to begin with a rather complex and lengthy (by Western standards) litany of inquiries that conveys interest in the other's individual and collective well-being and that reinforces the relationship between the two people. A Westerner might find this exchange cumbersome or even a waste of time, but it constitutes another way by which the fabric of collective society is knitted on a daily basis.

Does the continuous repetition of references to the influence of God over one's condition or actions reflect or shape a worldview that is fatalistic? Do people really believe that God determines every facet of their lives and every moment of the day? The answer is both yes and no. Perhaps a Muslim has received a kind and well-intentioned invitation that she or he knows is unlikely to be fulfilled. Instead of replying truthfully to the question "Can you come, will you please be there tonight?" with "No, I cannot make it, I am sorry," the invited person may respond "*Inshā' Allāh,* I will try to come tonight." This is a softer, less direct way of saying no, but it is one that relies on the well-understood set of phrases and meanings that places ultimate determination with God, but personal responsibility with the individual. Invitations to weddings, circumcision parties, or attendance at funeral gatherings are obligatory and are not subject to the nuance of "*Inshā' Allāh*". This is also understood.

When one is faced with a difficult situation, such as illness or financial trouble, friends will often comfort with the words, "*Allah Karīm*" (God will provide). This is a familiar phrase of comfort in the West as well and signals both resignation and an element of hope that the situation will improve. In the meantime action should be taken, a child should go to the doctor, or funds should be sought to relieve the immediate financial emergency. Sometimes a situation is so grave that a friend will comfort with the words, "There is little we can do, these things are out of our hands."

A sense of acceptance of one's fate is greater in some societies than in others. Folk Egyptian beliefs are well documented as accepting that one's life is foreordained or "written," as in the common expression that such and such is *maktūb*. Falling into the category of maktūb are such life events as one's marriage partner, or the number of children to be born and to survive, the death of family members and of oneself. There is little that is important in life that is accidental or not explained by a supernatural view of a grand plan. This is especially observed among Egyptian peasants (*fellaheen*) who have endured for millennia a marginal economic existence controlled more by outside forces or government than by themselves. It is this context, not a surprising worldview, that is likewise found among peasants throughout the world and is identified in anthropological texts as peasants' "image of the limited good".

However, among more urbanized, educated groups an attitude akin to fatalism is not usually expressed. Salma El-Jayussi, the great Palestinian poet and anthologizer of contemporary Arabic poetry, once told me that the most important thing that her mother told her was that her fate was in her hands. Likewise activist political movements—nationalist, feminist and even Islamist—today have taken the idea that social change rests in the hands of humans as agents of change. Although it can certainly be an advantage to claim God as an ally, such movements do not rely on the philosophy that God will provide, but are proactive, urgent, and very much of the moment.

Proverbs and Folk Wisdom

The Arabic language and Islamic culture are rich with proverbs and expressions that convey a worldview and sense of values that belongs to the realm of oral and folk traditions. Only a small selection of the large volume of sayings is offered here.

There are proverbs that comment on the universal human condition and the particular irony of the specialized craftsman going without the service he provides. From the Sudan comes, "The door of the carpenter is always broken" (*Bab al-najjar makhalla*), and in Tunisia, "Every shoe-maker goes barefoot" (*Kúl iskáfi hafi*). There is in these proverbs both a recognition of the importance of the service provided and the continuous labor necessary to make a living, such that one's own needs are neglected.

In the realm of consumer protection, to put a modern phrase to a bit of ancient wisdom, there is "Cheap becomes expensive and expensive is cheap" (*Rakhis ghali wa ghali rakhis*). In America we might say "you get what you pay for." Using the consumer idiom to talk about what you might buy in the butcher's market also has resonance in the challenges of everyday life: "In every piece of tender meat there is the bone" (*Kūl lahma fiha adma*). Or to put it in another English idiom, "Take the bad with the good."

In the realm of the maintenance of good social relations is the very wise "The most important thing about a house is its neighbors" (*Shoof al-jār qabal al-dār*), literally "look at the neighbors before the door of the house". This proverb stresses the importance of neighbors and commu-nity in its very definition of a good place to live. Indeed, according to Islamic law, a "good" house that a husband is obliged to provide for his wife is one that is not isolated and that is near to good neighbors.

An appreciation of difference and of changing times is found in the sage saying "For every time has its knowledge" (*Kūl saa' wa 'almha*). Another interpretation might be that every time period has its differing customs and ways and it is wrong to judge by current standards. A timeless sense of Egyptian endurance and fatalism is contained in the country's most famous saying, "And tomorrow there will be apricots" (*Wa bukra fi mish mish*), cynically meaning, in whatever the context, "you're dreaming."

4

Family, Community, and Gender Relations

A great deal of attention is being paid in the United States to a restoration of family values. In the space of a few decades in the United States we have moved from a time when the nuclear family was the dominant family form to a contemporary situation in which the subnuclear family, especially one comprised of divorced women and their children, has become an accepted and expected variant of the family. The extended family that dominated in agrarian times has long since been undermined by the Industrial Revolution, with its emphasis on the more compact, efficient, and mobile nuclear family. Family mobility has reached extensive proportions in the United States for the nuclear family, such that it is common to find parents and adult children separated geographically, as well as siblings who do not live near to one another and rarely see each other. The United States has among the highest rates of marital separation in the world, while remarriage and the blending of parts of former nuclear families after remarriage have presented new challenges to the definition of family structure.

Such dynamic reshaping of traditional conceptions of the family are fascinating to witness and study, but to the outside world, especially to the Muslim world, they may appear as baffling or even as alarming evidence of breakdown and decay. This is not to say that change is not impacting many parts of the traditional Arab and Muslim world and altering family patterns, but that change is slowed by limited industrialization, even though rapid urbanization has occurred in the past several decades. Religious revival, likewise, has made an issue of "family values" Muslim-style and has served to reinforce traditional family patterns.

Extended Family Life and Group Values

Despite widespread and rapid urbanization throughout the Arab and Muslim world, the extended family has not been fundamentally affected

59

to the degree that it has been displaced or even seriously challenged by the nuclear family. Even in the few examples that might be cited of shifting marriage and family patterns, the ideology of the extended family still predominates.

The Middle Eastern extended family has been aptly described as embracing both genealogical and physical closeness, a concept of family and nearness that is known in Arabic as *qaraba* (Eickelman 1989: 154). Typically, a traditional extended family occupies a part of a local neighborhood, known as a *hai,* and houses of extended families would be clustered near to one another. The relationships between houses and families would be patrilineal, according to Arab and Muslim custom, and a hai might include a grandfather or great uncle, their wives and families, father and mother, brothers, their wives and families, and perhaps cousins and their families related through patrilineal ties. A local household may include a paternal grandparent, uncle or aunt, unmarried siblings, or even a married brother or sister (though less frequent), and one's parents. A typical extended household may be comprised of all or part of several nuclear families. These days, with massive rural to urban migration, and expatriate migration for work, the extended family household is relied upon as a secure, stable place from which one may leave and to which one may always return. Urban extended households have become something of a way station for family migrants from rural homesteads as a means to become established in the city, as well as for ambitious urban migrants who come from poorer Muslim countries seeking lucrative jobs in richer Islamic countries. The social base from which these economic strategies can be launched has been and continues to be the extended family.

Qaraba, with its double meaning of physical nearness or intimacy and being related by kinship, can result in some confusion. I would often describe a person as being *qaribti,* or close to me, meaning that we are good friends; frequently I would be misinterpreted as describing a kinsperson, so I would add the descriptive noun "friend" or the explanatory phrase "like a sister." Likewise, the powerful kinship idiom pervades society and sometimes serves to soften or embellish impersonal relations. As one rides the buses, trains or other often crowded vehicles of public transportation in Cairo, you hear riders refer to the ticket collector as "Uncle" (*ya 'Amm*), or the conductor urging a crowd to make room for newcomers by referring to them as "my brothers" (*ya Ikhwani*).

Older women may address younger women in informal conversation as "my daughter" (*ya binti*), or women of more or less the same age might sprinkle their conversation with frequent use of "my sister" (*akhti*), as in "Am I not telling you the truth, *ya akhti?*"

For the anthropologist conducting research within an extended family, friendship or close association with one member of a family usually means that you will soon be visiting the family at home and getting to know siblings who are still at home, the parents, and other members of the extended family household. The individual is not separate from the family, and you become something like an extension of the family and may be addressed as "daughter" or "sister," or "brother." The hospitality that is offered freely and openly to members of the extended family, can also include outsiders, such as ourselves. During one of our research trips to the Sudan, Richard and I found it difficult to secure housing in Khartoum and were invited to stay with friends in Omdurman for as long as we needed. Our stay lasted for two months, included recuperation from malaria, and ended at our request once we had found a flat in Khartoum. The matter of offering payment for our stay would have been ridiculous and insulting, so the appropriate thanks was to bring specialty foods or gifts that would be enjoyed collectively. I noted that gifts that I had especially brought to individual friends were received collectively, so I eventually learned to present familial gifts that were nonessentials and could be used by all.

The social condition of the extended family provides not only shelter, food, and physical space for its individual members, but it contains within it a much broader ideology of mutual support and solidarity for the family group. The idea of family (*'ā'ila*) is so engrained and powerful that it is rarely invoked inside the family, as it might be in the West where a family member is called upon to do something "for the sake of the family" or family name. Family is everything; there is no need to stress its importance to those who are well aware of the fact. *'Ā'ila* then is a term that is used more outside of the family in reference to it, such as identifying family members to inquiring anthropologists, for example. One of the kindest and most endearing ways of saying good-bye to a close friend, especially popular in Egypt, is that "you are from my family" (*Inta min ahali*), or in Sudan, "We are as one family" (*Nehnah 'ā'ila wahda*). It is an extension of a powerful kinship idiom to one who has been afforded the status of being like a sister or brother.

With the support that the extended family provides to its members comes responsibility as well. A family that may have pooled its resources to send a talented member to university at home or abroad bestows upon the recipient family member a responsibility to return a measure of what he or she has received (the recipient is most likely to be male and the burden falls more heavily upon the male than upon the female). Returning from the city where one has studied, or from abroad where one has worked or studied, one carries extra suitcases full of gifts or goods that will be absorbed by the household. Items that are not readily available locally or are too expensive such as kitchen appliances, household decorations, or portable radios and televisions, are commonly presented to the household. Long stays and successful careers mean that large items, such as refrigerators or VCRs, may be purchased and given to the household. Gifts brought to individual family members, such as a favorite sister, are in another category of special affection and are not part of the generalized system of reciprocity that functions in the extended family.

Sometimes individuals from extended family backgrounds who have spent long periods of time away, or have made new homes in the West, fear or are apprehensive about returning home because of the strong family bonds that they may perceive as tying them down or that they feel burden them with a sense of responsibility that they may not be able to meet. Money may be loaned or given to family members with little expectation of return on either side. Often unrealistic images of material success, especially of one returning from a Western, industrialized country, may make visits home awkward for the struggling student or immigrant worker. The point is that the extended family has provided the background for whatever success has been achieved, and there is a powerful understood value of reciprocity for sharing whatever success has been achieved.

Patrilineal Kinship and the Extended Family

Patrilineality, or descent and inheritance traced through males, characterizes Arab and Islamic society. The core group of patrilineally related males are known collectively as the 'asaba, and they constitute the most prominent figures in the descent system and extended family. They are also the key decision-makers for important family affairs. The 'asaba

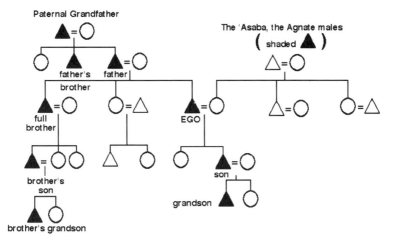

Fig. 3. Diagram of the 'Asaba, core group of males in patrilineal Arab Muslim society. From *Islamic Law and Society in the Sudan* by Carolyn Fluehr-Lobban. London: Frank Cass, 1987. Reprinted by permission of the publisher.

then includes: the paternal grandfather, the father, the son, the paternal uncles, their sons, and so on. Following the logic of patrilineal descent, males both inherit and bestow patrilineal descent, whereas females inherit but do not convey patrilineal descent. It is important to recognize that females are not excluded from patrilineal descent.

The 'asaba includes the real and symbolic heads of respective extended family segments, and of the corporate family grouping that constitutes the lineage. These are men who, accordingly, receive a high degree of respect and deference from their family members, from women in general, and from younger males. As formal figures of authority the 'asaba are deferred to in family decision making, particularly marriage and financial matters. While there is a great deal of informal decision-making that goes on in families, the formal, public role falls to the father, as head of the household, or to a member of the 'asaba. Younger males typically do not speak first in the presence of older men, or they wait until they are addressed; they do not smoke in the company of the older 'asaba, or they might ask permission before lighting a cigarette. One of the marks of a progressive family is the degree to which there is an open and free exchange of ideas among family members, free of the traditional hierarchy of 'asaba, younger men, and women.

A strong complement to patrilineal descent in many Arab and Islamic societies is a custom of patrilocal residence, in which the newly married couple takes up residence with or near to the groom's family. It is the bride who leaves her home to join her husband. However, she does not join her husband's patrilineage and always remains a member of her father's patrilineal group, from which she will ultimately inherit. Her identity throughout life is that to which she was born, as in *Fāṭima bint Muḥammad*, Fāṭima the daughter of Muḥammad. She does not take her husband's name, but her children are born to their father's patrilineage and take the name of their father. In the event of divorce or death of her husband, or any other difficulty, she is always welcome, even expected, to return to the house of her father. Her young children are legally in her care and custody until they reach prescribed ages of majority at which time they are claimed by the patrilineal descent group into which they were born.

Family and lineage represent the largest measure of one's identity. Families are a part of lineages that comprise the lengthy history and genealogy of a people, known as *nasab*. This nasab, the long line of upright and religious ancestors traced patrilineally, is a source of pride in one's heritage and placement in the larger society. The right conduct and achievments of individuals are generalized to the level of the extended family and are a part of informal public knowledge and discussion. Even in large cities, the importance of the identity of family and lineage is not lost and is a part of everyday life affecting just about any institution from business, to education, to politics. As such many activities are carried out on a personal basis through contacts that are made between and through networks of extended families. Being a part of this complex network may ensure the best price in the purchase of an expensive appliance or car, admission to a university, less time or money spent in a legal matter or with a cumbersome bureaucracy, or access to otherwise unavailable services or purchases, such as desirable airline fares or tickets. Such favors again fall into the category of generalized reciprocity whereby family members and their friends do for each other, with a general expectation of return but without any specified cost accounting. In these ways and a thousand others, Arab and Muslim society operates in a highly personalized context, making even the most urban setting less impersonal. It is frequently remarked of the world's Arab and Islamic cities that they are really clusters of villages, that is, groups of extended families concentrated in the city's neighborhoods.

High-status families are notable, as they are in other parts of the world, and are expected to perform in exceptional ways. Even their mediocre members are elevated by membership in a well-known family. In contrast, individuals from low-status families may have to over-achieve in order to receive equal recognition. These patterns, based in old class divisions and ideas about family honor, are quite conservative and resistant to change in brief periods of time such as a generation or two. The notion of rapid and unlimited social mobility, which we in parts of the West believe exists as a reward for hard work and merit, is generally not part of this worldview. As long as one has an attachment to family and lineage one is secure; without it life, not to mention success in life, is in serious jeopardy.

Marriage Patterns

Marriage is the central institution around which all other social and kin institutions revolve, and it is guarded and protected by the 'asaba and revered by the entire social group. It is never taken lightly, and elaborate formal negotiations precede its contracting. Its celebratory rituals form the centerpiece of music, dance and folklore. Marriage is the single most important event in the life of a man or woman; the ties that are created through marriage are so important that, traditionally, decisions regarding choice of marriage partner were rarely, if ever, left to the future bride or groom alone.

Endogamy, or marriage within the larger extended family, is extremely common, with the preferred marriage partner being the male's first cousin on the father's side, (bint 'amm, or the father's brother's daughter). In some traditional communities bint 'amm marriage may reach as high as 40 percent of all marriages (Lobban 1982); whether its frequency is high or low, it has persisted as the preferred marriage form even in highly urbanized communities. In Cairo, for example, first-cousin marriage remains the most common marital form, whether the marriage partner is father's brother's daughter or some other paternal first cousin or, failing this, a first cousin on the mother's side. Rugh (1984) notes that the preference for cousin marriage is still so powerful in Egypt that families may disguise the fact of non-cousin marriage. In one sample of 500 Sudanese women in Omdurman, 60 percent had married their first cousins from within their families (Grotberg and Washi 1991).

Sudanese couple who married in traditional fashion; she is his father's brother's daughter.

Explanations for this marriage preference are both economic and social. By keeping marriage within the extended family, wealth and property are thereby consolidated within the kin group. "Stranger" marriage, which is considered very risky, is controlled. By contrast, the more traditional bint 'amm marriage is given strong support by extended family members, so that these marriages tend to be more stable and less likely to end in divorce or separation. The families, of course, know each other well and trust in marriage negotiations and subsequent relations is high, unlike the situation with "stranger" marriage.

Students in the West often ask about the possibility of genetic or biological abnormalities that may result from relatively close inbreeding. First-cousin marriage is generally prohibited by law in the United States, although various states have differing laws regarding the marriage of second cousins. Systematic study of the biological effects of this marriage-breeding pattern has not been conducted. But my observation of families in which the rate of bint 'amm marriage is among the highest, for example among the Tuti Islanders of Khartoum, did not reveal any obvious problems or anomalies. Moreover, even if some genetic disadvantage in first-cousin marriage were demonstrated, probably few families would make any dramatic change, because the perceived value of such marriages is so high. Indeed, in the recent period of accelerated class formation, endogamous marriage has been reinforced as a way to keep newly acquired wealth within the family's control.

Protecting the selection of a woman's marriage partner is the responsibility of the marriage guardian (al-wāli), who is most often the father or some other close male, paternal kin. In traditional times women rarely contested the choice of spouse, but legal reform in the twentieth century has moved to ensure the consent of the bride to the marriage and has offered interpretations of how, exactly, consent is given. In these more complex times, greater numbers of brides are protesting marriage proposals, persuading their fathers to favor their choices, or seeking legal remedies in court to prevent their fathers from forcing them into unwanted marriages.

Exogamous marriage, or marriage outside of the broadly interpreted patrilineal kin group, is thus defined as "stranger" marriage. Proposals of marriage that have not been negotiated by the natural marriage guardians, the 'asaba, but have been initiated by the couple themselves are still exceptional and relatively rare. The couple may have become acquainted at the university or at the place of employment. Such a couple must approach their elders for approval. If it is given, and before it is given, the family will inquire and gather relevant information about the background of the family with which they are about to be united. Relevant questions would touch upon economic background and whether they are more or less equivalent in status, appropriate religious commonalities in piety and practice, the family's background and history (nasab), and other matters that place the two families on an equal footing in the proposed union. The appropriate match of families is known as

Sudanese couple who married in nontraditional fashion, choosing one another as marriage partners.

"equality of standard in marriage" (*al-Kafa'a fil zawāj*) and has been a powerful social tradition that has kept marriage not only within families, but within class and religious community as well. Proposals of marriage between families who know one another due to business or community ties are certainly considered less risky than marriage proposals made by individuals who became acquainted by chance in some anonymous place.

The Western idea of falling in love with someone whom you met casually at a bus stop, at a cafe, or, perish the thought, at a singles bar, is considered dangerous and barbaric. How can the couple possibly know what they are getting into without the appropriate social controls? "Stranger" marriage that has been opposed by one or both of the families represents the greatest challenge to the couple, who may have to resort to a Shari'a court judge to act as marriage guardian for the woman and approve the marriage. Without familial support, they face many financial and emotional difficulties, and statistically, these are the least stable marriages.

Marriage is not legal without a negotiated dower known as *mahr*, nor without a negotiated contract, the *'aqd*. The dower is a large sum of money or wealth in property that is owed to the bride by the groom from the time of the signing of the marriage contract. The negotiated dower is usually large, in comparison with the family's status, so that the groom often negotiates payment in "prompt" and "deferred" amounts. The total amount of the dower may be thousands or tens of thousands of dollars for a middle-class marriage. Some of the Islamist resurgence movements in Tunisia, the Sudan and elsewhere have criticized the inflationary dower costs and have reformed the social practice to the negotiation of a one-dinar or one-pound dower.

The dower has become so high that men may be forced to postpone marriage into their late twenties and thirties, until they have accumulated sufficient funds for prompt payment, as well as for the house and furnishings they must also provide. A significant number of the young male laborers who migrate from the poor Arab countries to the oil rich nations are temporary workers saving their money for marriage.

The Islamic dower, which is made as a legal debt of the groom to the bride, is probably a reform of pre-Islamic patrilineal bridewealth negotiations, whereby wealth was exchanged between families. Making the large amount of wealth represented in the dower payable to the woman guarantees her economic security and protection in the marriage. It is likewise an insurance against divorce, since the full amount of the negotiated dower must be paid at the time of the husband's divorce of the wife. While the husband has the sole financial responsibility of the wife and children, the wife has the responsibility to bear and rear the children of the husband's patrilineage, and she owes to her husband obedience, which is defined as cohabitation. The fathers and the paternal uncles of the groom occasionally help with the financial arrangements. The father of the bride sometimes receives, as a voluntary offering, or takes as a paternal authority part of her dower payment. But to do so invites social criticism because such behavior by a father is considered unmanly.

The 'aqd, or contract signing, is the legal beginning of the marriage, but it usually precedes actual cohabitation by about six months or a year. Anything that is not contrary to Islam and is mutually agreed upon can be put into the marriage contract. This might include a clause on monogamy, or a mutual agreement about child custody in the event of divorce or death. The contract signing ceremony is a simple affair that is a culmination of marriage negotiations. For all but the most conservative families, the period after the 'aqd is the time when the "engaged" couple can actually go out together and get to know each other better. If problems develop in this period before cohabitation, then a negotiated divorce can be effected with little permanent consequence to either party.

Dating, as we know it in the West, does not exist in Arab-Islamic society, nor do young people have the opportunities for sexual adventures. Controls on premarital sexuality are very rigid, and the idea that a young person might have his or her own apartment is out of the question. Dormitories at universities are segregated by sex, or students live at home with their parents. There are few places where men and women mix freely, and where it is socially acceptable, such mixed gatherings are in private homes under the watchful eyes of parents and guardians. Weddings are joyous occasions where young people are given a greater degree of freedom to interact, flirt, or perhaps dance in each other's presence. Hotels are very strict about proof of marriage before renting their rooms to couples, and many of the urban areas where prostitution once may have flourished have now been cleansed of such moral corruption by Islamist activism. Young men, who leave home to go to other countries for work or further education, have greater freedom for sexual experimentation, which is dangerous and shameful for a young woman. Virginity is demanded of a woman at the time of her first marriage, but it is not unusual for the less traveled groom also to be a virgin on his wedding night.

Weddings celebrate the couple beginning to live together, and they are and have been historically elaborate affairs that constitute the centerpiece of family and community life and folklore. Traditional weddings lasted for three to seven days, including rituals associated with henna dying of the bride's hands and feet, symbolic visits of the groom's kin to the bride's family and vice versa, feasting, music and dancing, culminating in the final "night of entry" (*lailat al-dukhla*) when the groom and entourage come to the bride's house and, after much celebration and ritual symbolizing the union of the couple and the two families, the marriage is consummated. The urban version of the marriage celebration preceeding cohabitation is the occasion for the large public gathering of family and friends, often in one of the major hotels equipped for large parties. The contemporary bride often wears a white bridal gown of Western inspiration, but many Muslim couples are choosing to have less-flamboyant weddings and simpler, more culturally authentic wedding costumes.

Some couples will spend a period away on a honeymoon, although the idea is clearly a Western import, as is the photograph in the white dress that some brides insist upon. Others use the wedding as an opportunity to begin a new life in a new place, perhaps outside of their city or country. In traditional marriages the couple takes up residence patrilocally, with the groom's family, where the young wife adapts to her new role as daughter-in-law. Very few couples live neolocally, that is apart from either family. Nubians in Egypt and the Sudan vary this strictly patrilineal-patrilocal pattern with a period of matrilocal residence with the wife's family, from as little as forty days to the time of the birth of the first child, expected within the first year of marriage. This may be a remnant of the prior matrilineal descent that prevailed in Nubia until the introduction of Islam.

If the marriage ends, either by divorce or death, the wife must pass three monthly courses, if she is still menstruating, for a period of time known as the *'idda*. This ensures that she is not pregnant and is therefore free to marry again. However, if she is pregnant, both she and the child are protected by law to ensure their continued support by the former husband. Many people in the Middle East are surprised to find that nothing like the *'idda* is practiced in the West. They realize that, theoretically at least, non-Muslims can divorce on one day and remarry the next, but they worry about the possibility of pregnancy from the previous marriage impinging on the new marriage, as well as about how the nasab of the child will be protected.

Marriage is the normal state for men and women, and someone who has remained unmarried is either pitied or thought of as somehow strange. Preference for the married state is clearly stated in the Qur'ān, and it is a major preoccupation in Arab and Muslim society as the main vehicle by which families and communities are bound in all important networks of mutual interest.

Inheritance Patterns

Inheritance follows a modified form of patrilineal transmission of wealth and property that is prescribed by Islam. The heirs in Muslim family law are outlined in the Qur'ān, are therefore defined religiously, and are not subject to very much in the way of human interpretation. These prescribed heirs include the father/mother, the grandfather/grandmother, the son/daughter, with as a general principle the patrilineal kin being favored over relations through the mother's side, and blood or consanguinal relations favored over affines (relatives by marriage).

Again, the 'asaba is the core group through whom inheritance passes, although their role is as much one of guardianship and protector of the family wealth and property as it is one of direct inheritance. Lineal relatives (parents, grandparents, children) are favored over collaterals (aunts, uncles, cousins) in inheritance, and males are favored over females. The rationale for the former principle is the strengthening of the lineal ties from father to son to grandson, while the reason for the latter principle is that females, who are supported by their male kin, have less financial need and no economic responsibilites toward their kinspeople. Where males and females are in equal structural positions in the kinship system, such as with brothers and sisters, males are entitled to twice what their sisters inherit. Because women are also supported by their husbands, even when they have independent means of income, there has been little feminist objection to this apparent discrimination against women. Where Muslim familiy law is applied to non-Muslims, such as in Egypt where a significant Coptic minority is governed by general Egyptian law, there has been outspoken criticism of the inequitable treatment of males and females in inheritance law.

Family wealth that is controlled by the 'asaba often consists of its immovable property, such as land, date trees, or houses. Although individual shares of this wealth may be inherited, there is a strong sense of corporate ownership among kinspeople, which makes infrequent the sale or transference of immovable property. Movable wealth, such as money, animals, or jewelry is less protected by the corporate responsibilities of the 'asaba and is inherited more on an individual basis.

There can be differences of opinion among the 'asaba regarding the disposition of inherited immovable wealth, such as land. Traditional family land may have increased greatly in value by virtue of its proximity to an urban area; what once was valuable agricultural land is now worth more due to real estate speculation. It may be difficult to achieve unanimity as to the future disposition of the inherited land among the corporate 'asaba and a conservative position to do nothing may prevail.

Individual gifts to family members can be made outside of the prerogatives and laws of Qur'ānic inheritance. Such gifts, known as *hiba*, can be made for the disposition of valued and sentimental property, such as a family heirloom, or for a special purpose, such as on the occasion of the marriage of a daughter or son. They fall outside of the intent of the general principles of Islamic inheritance if such gifts favor inequitably one heir over another. Likewise charitable trusts, *waqfs* (discussed below) made in perpetuity for some social benefit may not be used as a way of disinheriting heirs, nor can they be used for increasing the share of an heir.

Islamic family law permits one to bequeath wealth and property to non-Qur'ānic heirs and to increase the shares of Qur'ānic heirs by means of a will, up to one-third of an estate. The larger two-thirds must be bequeathed to the entitled heirs, making it impossible to disinherit relatives entitled under Islamic prescriptions. This religiously based system of inheritance has had the effect of avoiding feuds and controlling disputes over the disposition of family wealth among kinspeople. Coming as I do from a Western family that has been divided for three generations over disagreements resulting from the distribution of inherited wealth, I can appreciate a system that has specific and predictable rules and makes illegal the disinheriting of legal and entitled heirs.

Bequests in the name of God (*waqf*, pl. *awqaf*), usually for communal religious purposes, have historically been an important part of Muslim inheritance. These bequests are typically made outside of the immediate family, but generally serve to benefit the local community. A parcel of land set aside in holy trust for the construction of a mosque or school can be nominated as a *waqf*, or funds to maintain or expand a mosque or hospital can be similarly nominated. The intent of the donor must be clearly declared and recorded so that the heirs are informed and are not unfairly treated through this mechanism, intended for social good and not for family retribution through denial of inheritance.

Illegitimacy: To Be without Ancestry or Genealogy

To be without attachment to a patrilineage or a genealogy, without nasab, is virtually not to exist, and it is one of the worst conditions that can befall a Muslim. The social repercussions of illegitimacy are profound and so far reaching as to haunt the mother, her family, and the child for their entire lives. The societal cost is so high that other mechanisms have intervened to mollify the effects on the children and to give the pregnant mother every benefit of the doubt. Māliki interpretation of the Muslim family law regarding legitimacy traditionally permitted four years to pass after death or divorce by a husband, during which legitimacy of the former husband's patrilineage would pass to a child born after their separation. Later interpretations, accepted by majority legal opinion, recognize a period of one year as sufficient to bestow legitimacy on any child born after separation, death, or divorce by the husband. This liberal interpretation of parentage, especially fatherhood, underscores the critical importance of nasab, of having a place in the social scheme of things defined as patrilineal ties.

The shame attached to illegitimacy is so great for the mother, as proof of her sexual misconduct, and for the child, born without legal tie to the father, that destruction of the infant may appear to be the only solution. This particular form of infanticide exists in conjunction with the idea of family honor and eliminating the shame of bearing an illegitimate child.

Cases that I have knowledge of where a woman has born an illegitimate child and has raised it on her own are rare and often tragic. The social stigma is great and may be insurmountable by a woman alone. She may be driven from place to place unable to keep long-term employment, or she may be forced to seek the anonymity of expatriation. Seeking the aid of kinspeople and raising the child with the mother's family is a solution, but one that makes the shame of the birth a constant reminder and may result in ill-treatment of the child.

Beyond these facts, legal adoption is difficult and virtually impossible in Islamic courts of law. Legitimacy is only conveyed through nasab, and nasab is conferred through legitimate marriage or by an admission of paternity in a court of law, with its attendant responsibilities. There is no notion of adoptive paternity in Islamic law, and the fundamental criterion of legitimacy derives from the conception of a child during the lawful wedlock of its parents (Coulson 1971: 23).

For a childless couple, "burden of proof" usually falls to the woman as the one responsible for infertility. Barrenness is one of the acceptable grounds for taking a second wife, even in today's reformed practice of polygyny.

While legal adoption is impossible in Islamic family law, informal fosterage is actually quite common. For an extended family, already a communal unit, to take in a child is not a serious logistical problem, as it would be where nuclear family norms prevail and individual privacy is a priority. The agreement to raise a child not biologically a member of the patrilineage is seen as a matter of human compassion and does not affect the patterns of inheritance. A child may be taken in because of some misfortune or death that has befallen its parents, perhaps in some other part of the country where the father of the extended family conducts business.

War and economic strife, such as the Sudan has experienced in the past several decades, has created many economically stranded individuals or orphans in its wake; a few of these displaced children, Muslim or not, may be taken in and raised by a Muslim family. Naturally the child would then be socialized to Arab and Muslim ways. While children raised in such a way do not acquire entitlement to patrilineal descent and inheritance, they do become associated with the household as part of its daily activities, work routines, and socializing. The child is often educated with the biological children, but may need a family protector to keep older siblings or others from temptations of verbal or physical abuse or demands for servile behavior. The lack of a mechanism for formal legal adoption creates an ambiguous status for the fostered child and might engender inequitable treatment.

In cases where the child has been happily and successfully assimilated into the family, inheritance in the form of a special bequest or legal gift may be given to this fostered child of the family. Arab history and folklore is replete with "sons" who have been adopted in this way, especially by childless fathers or fathers without sons.

Fosterage as a specialized topic in Islamic law deals with the legal ramifications of the relationship established between non-kin individuals where a woman has suckled a child who is not her own. According to Sharī'a, the children of the mother who nursed such a child and her own biological children are as brothers and sisters. They are subject to the same incest and marriage taboos as brothers and sisters and cannot marry one another. This is the rather specialized meaning of fosterage in Islamic society.

The well-known American international aid association Foster Parents Plan changed its name to Plan, International, primarily because of the difficulties it was having translating the concept of foster parents into a Muslim context. Having a specialized meaning for fosterage yet lacking a mechanism for adoption, the translation of the term *foster parents* became awkward and socially inept, and so the change was made in order the make the program viable in Muslim areas.

The whole subject of legitimacy, nasab, and fosterage is sensitive in Islamic society, and perhaps in its negation, it reflects the crucial importance of the patrilineal kin group and the sense of place it gives the individual in the grandest scheme of things.

Male-Female Relations, Patriarchal Traditions, and their Limitations

Islamic society was constructed upon Arab society that had developed strong patrilineal traditions in Arabia before the advent of Islam. Patrilineality is commonly found among pastoral peoples practicing traditional economy of pre-Islamic Arabia. With the growth of towns and widening trade networks, patrilineal kinship ties were utilized to extend commercial linkages, and patriarchal ideas were borrowed from neighboring societies or developed independently as an outgrowth of urban society and patrilineal descent.

Patriarchical social relations are most probably not original with the Arabs, but developed in the context of the formation of the state in pre-Semitic, regional Mesopotamian culture. The Babylonian Code of Hammurabi includes control of female sexuality and reproduction before and within marriage, which can be readily adjudged as the enforcement of patriarchical traditions already well established (Lerner 1986). A strong case can be made that Islam brought about a degree of reform improving the status of women within a long standing patriarchal society.

While the West finds it easy to condemn patriarchy in Arab and Islamic society, it rarely is able to see the patriarchal roots and continuing expressions of patriarchy in its more familiar Christian and Judaic customs derived from the same roots. The controversies over the training and annointing of women as rabbis, priests, or church officials is one of many cases in point. Although stemming from a common religious and cultural foundation in the Middle East, Islamic society has been singled out in the West as a worst case example of the low status and poor treatmemnt of women. Its women are held to be universally veiled, subordinated, and passive nonparticipants in society who are to be pitied, unlike their male counterparts who are either to be feared (as potential terrorists) or reviled. The realities, like so much else in the story of Arab-Islamic society, is vastly different from the mythology.

Male-Female Relations

Within a society so shaped by patrilineal institutions and patriarchal traditions, it is not surprising that the most important gender relationships that have been constructed are between men and groups of men. Male relatives, who may also be neighbors or live close by, possess strong bonds of kinship and friendship. The latter dimension often surprises Westerners, who may find that these kinsmen are often also the closest of comrades and friends. When these bonds are broken by offense, insult, or disloyalty, the hurt is great and efforts to mend relations go well beyond the feuding parties. Reconciliation may take place in the name of the family and for the good of the family.

Traditionally, the closest personal bonding takes place within the extended family along gender lines. Women who are related to each other patrilineally as daughters and sisters and women who have married into the family, who may also be cousins, form a close network of associates, friends, and confidantes. Because most women are still not employed outside of the home, a majority spend their adult, married lives in the domestic arena in the close company of other women.

Safeguarding the honor of families and the respectability of women is a continuous preoccupation in male-female relations, so there are settings where it is proper and generally permissable for males and females to mix and others that are more constrained. Public arenas may be mixed or sexually segregated, depending upon local traditions and rural-urban differences. Public transportation may be relaxed and mixed, as in Tunisia, or it can be sexually segregated, as in the Muslim Sudan, where women and men sit separately. In highly congested Cairo, where public transport is likely to be crowded, the close physical contact makes voluntary sexual separation a frequent choice for males and females. Dressing in conservative Islamist fashion adds a measure of protection for women. In my own case, bringing a child with me on the bus or train provided the additional protection that would offset possible curiosity or stereotyping of Western women. Rural areas are likely to be more relaxed about male-female interaction in public places than are semiurban or urban areas.

Public education is usually sex-segregated at elementary and secondary levels and coeducational at the university level. Male and female teachers are represented at each level. However, like the West, the teaching of younger children tends to be dominated by females. One of the major trends of twentieth century education in the Muslim world has been the increasing numbers of females represented, not only in elementary grades, but also in secondary and postsecondary education. Many major universities, like Cairo University, now have about 50 percent female students.

The university is a public place where males and females easily mix in classrooms, in the university environment in general, and in other public lecture sites. Outside of the university a more conservative pattern prevails, although under the influence of Islamist activism, universities are experiencing a voluntary resegregation. Still, the university remains one of the few places outside of the family where respectable interaction between unrelated males and females can take place without fear of gossip or intimidation.

Weddings are another arena wherein young women and men can meet socially, converse, even flirt, and in some cultural traditions, dance together. They are under the watchful eyes of their adult relatives, but the relaxed and celebratory atmosphere of the wedding party provides a unique opportunity for unmarried young people to socialize and be in closer contact than society normally permits. Weddings are thus very popular events and are typically large social affairs.

Male-female interactions that are improper or forbidden include all forms of dating before a couple has contracted marriage (or become "engaged"). Meeting at a cafe or a restaurant is not proper, and all but the most westernized couples aver such a rendezvous. Even in the most westernized suburbs of major cities, discreet, secluded areas of a cafe may be reserved for mixed couples; only the tourist hotels catering almost exclusively to Westerners deviate from this pattern. Movie going as a cultural import from the West has historically been a male-dominated recreation, but increasingly more engaged or married couples are attending. Many movie theaters provide sections for unescorted women, or women attend the cinema during matinee hours when fewer males are present.

Situations where an unrelated male and female may be left alone together are also avoided, as the cultural presumption is that something of a sexual nature may occur between them. A male physician may not examine a woman without a third party present, usually a husband or close male relative or a nurse. This cultural tradition of protection and modesty is so strong that it alone constitutes a sufficient argument for the training of more female physicians.

To the casual Western observer, men are more visible in urban areas as they tend to congregate publicly in coffee houses and restaurants in downtown areas. When large numbers of men are visible during day-time hours, it suggests high unemployment, and the topic of conversation over endless cups of Arabic coffee is likely to be the job shortage or the possibility of emigration to a richer Arab country or to Europe. A high degree of mutual assistance and male solidarity is thus promoted where the focus is on male-male interaction without the diversion of women. Such coffeehouses have historically been places where political discussions flourished and activism naturally followed. It has flowed from this that the streets are public domain and thus the provenance of men. When women have joined with men in the streets in public demonstrations around nationalist or more recently Islamist activism, their participation is that much more dramatic.

Men's closest friends are men, and it is more often with men that their feelings flow with the recitation of poetry or the appreciation of a favorite singer or musician. In some cultural contexts drinking of alcoholic beverages has provided another context for male bonding, even though this behavior is anathema to Islam. Having friendships with unrelated females is quite rare, and when they exist it is often the result of a progressive ideology or some exposure to non-Muslim society. As a foreign woman I had some flexibility to develop friendships with men, but relations were always more restrained with me than with my husband. Close male-female bonding within the family is more likely to exist between a brother and sister than between a husband and wife. Men and women do not marry for closeness and intimacy, as they do in the West. Husbands and wives will not walk down the street holding hands, but it is not uncommon to see two men walking hand-in-hand or to see men embrace one another and kiss as they meet on the street. To the casual Western observer this may appear unmasculine, as men in the West are socialized to be restrained in the company of other men and to shake hands rather than embrace and kiss. Although bravery and honor are extolled as male virtues, so also are poetry and expressive singing which reveal another side of men.

Women, likewise, form their closest relationships with other women who are relatives, neighbors, or friends, as age-mates from school or other activities. Visiting and countervisiting in each other's homes, possibly in the *hareem,* or women's section of the home, is almost continuous. When life allows a more leisurely pace, women spend long hours together socializing in the context of simple visiting or working together in some domestic task, such as food preparation or sewing. Pure relaxation among women occurs in the context of some cosmetic rituals, such as lengthy sessions of hair-braiding or elaborate decorating of the hands and feet with henna dye. More often than not these sessions take place in preparation for a wedding or some other important occasion, such as the birth or circumcision of a child, and they have the double function of accomplishing a task and cementing female relationships. These informal sessions are lighthearted, open and fair game for the discussion of any subject from sex and marriage, to birth control, to the economy, to the personal lives of those known to the group. It was in this sort of group setting that I learned the Arabic language and the multiple social meanings of many words and phrases. This intimacy takes place in the privacy of homes, and it is rare to see women out together socializing in public in a cafe or restaurant. The streets in the Arab-Muslim city are the province of men.

It is also in these group social settings that they exchange important information regarding their rights in marriage and divorce, and where strategies are worked out for women having problems in certain areas of their lives. A woman whose family is experiencing economic difficulty may discuss possible ways of earning money without losing her respectability. Another, having problems with her husband, may seek advice as to who among her male relatives might intercede on her behalf with her husband or his relatives. Informal discussion of arranged marriages may take place first among women before it is approached or negotiated by the male 'asaba. Determining that a young woman is interested in a suggested marriage and would give her consent to it often takes place in the hareem before any public announcement occurs.

Women rely on one another for social support in public and prefer to go out together for shopping or other errands in small groups. Like men, women can be seen walking together arm-in-arm occupying a closer physical space than is customary for westerners. Women who are strangers may stand together waiting in line at a bank or office, or women may be waited on first as a courtesy and a means of avoiding public scrutiny of a woman alone. The increasing participation of women in the labor force has necessitated modification of traditional patterns of sex segregation.

The Changing Status of Women

For the professional woman or the political activist, of which there are many, her movements are shaped by this general framework. Her primary identity is with her family; her closest ties are with other women; and her professional or activist life is protected by these associations. Major change affecting the status of women has occurred in virtually every Muslim and Arab nation and has been strongly associated with the nationalist movements and the first decades of independence.

In every instance where colonialism was resisted and political movements shaped the new national identity, women played their part. Together with men they organized demonstrations for national self-determination in every former colony, with notable well-documented cases in Egypt, Algeria, and among the Palestinians. Hoda Shar'awi and Ceza Nabarawi became internationally recognized symbols of the Arab-Muslim's women's struggle when they returned from Europe and reentered Egypt as unveiled, emancipated women. Understanding the sensitive and complex set of values associated with veiling, they organized nationalist and feminist demonstrations comprised of both unveiled and veiled women. To be sure, these pioneering Muslim feminists were highly educated and generally upper-class Egyptian women, but they forged an Arab-Muslim women's agenda that was intended to transform society once independence was achieved. That agenda included the promotion of female education at all levels, including the opening up of the professions to women; the acceptance of women participating in the public spheres of life; reform of certain of the family laws, especially the divorce laws; and suffrage for women.

In Algeria, where a war of national liberation against France was necessary to achieve independence, women participated as collaboraters in the armed struggle, carrying political leaflets and weapons under their veils. This heroic involvement of women is well-documented in the film, *The Battle of Algiers*. The French colonial authorities, seeking to undermine this political use of the veil and project themselves as the emancipators of women, conducted humiliating public unveilings during the last years of the armed struggle. The predictable effect was reinforcement of the cultural meaning of the veil as Algerian and Islamic, and with the success of the nationalist movement women returned to the wearing of the veil on a mass scale. Also, it might be added somewhat cynically that men took power and were reluctant to share it with the women alongside whom they had struggled for national independence.

The mobilization of women initially around the issue of nationalism, with the addition of a feminist agenda, was a scenario that was replayed in a number of less well known, but nevertheless dramatic and courageous historical examples. These include the now documented cases of the Sudan and Tunisia (Fluehr-Lobban 1977, 1981; Labidi 1990; Tessler 1978), the Yemen and Iraq, Syria and Lebanon (Beck and Keddie 1978; Haddad 1984). While in no instance did women come to power after independence, the agenda for social change was broadly accepted and implemented. Women have the right to vote in virtually every Arab-Muslim country, with the exception of feudal kingdoms, such as Saudi Arabia and Kuwait, which experienced neither direct colonialism nor concomitant struggles for independence. In the late 1980s Benazir Bhutto became the first woman to head an Islamic Republic, in Pakistan. Education for women has expanded from elementary to higher education. Contemporary Islamist movements also strongly endorse education for women, as their secular predecessors did, and a significant proportion of the Islamist activists are women students. The professions have been opened for women and it is quite ordinary to meet a woman medical doctor, engineer, lawyer, or university professor. In fact, women comprised a greater proportion of medical doctors and engineers in the Middle East than they did in the West until very recent times. The conflicts between career and family are not as acute as they are in the West due to the continued strength of the extended family and its ability to care for children at home, as well as the availability of affordable daycare.

A number of women in Egypt, the Sudan, Tunisia, Iraq, Jordan, Syria, and Lebanon have been appointed to important ministerial posts or have been elected to public office within their respective governments, while others have served as their nation's ambassadors abroad or at the United Nations. The influential Egyptian television industry is dominated by female employees and has numerous female officials at the top of this massive enterprise. The so-called glass ceiling, much commented upon in the United States as blocking women's achievement of the highest levels of government or business hierarchies, has not been as much of a barrier in these nations.

The appropriate status of women today is a much-debated issue in the context of Islamic revival, as the earlier secular models of society are increasingly being challenged. This and other debates and tensions within contemporary Islamic society are taken up in chapter 7.

5

Communal Identity: Religious, Ethnic, National

The focus of this book is on Islamic society and the culture and values it promotes where it has extended its influence. Islam originated within Arab culture and spread throughout southwest Asia, North Africa, and the Iberian Peninsula within its first century, and it was absorbed in succeeding centuries by cultures from eastern Asia westward to the African continent and to North America. Obviously there is no single ethnicity attached to Islam, although there is the powerful, overriding concept of the Umma, the world community of believers, that does convey a supraethnic, transnational identity for the nearly one billion people who profess Islam. And in terms of ethnic identity, there is no question that Arab culture and the Arabic language have played major roles in the shaping of the religion of Islam and "cultural" identity that it conveys.

In the last chapter I dwelt on the communal identity at the microlevel that is drawn from one's relationship to extended families and local community; in this chapter I focus on communal identity at the macrolevel—ethnic, national, and regional. The way that one's identity is constructed in relation to others, others who are defined as outsiders to one's immediate social group but nevertheless are co-citizens in contemporary nation-states, and others defined as foreigners, Muslim and non-Muslim—the sorting out of religion, ethnicity and nation is the subject of this chapter.

Religious Identity

In many regions where the Islamic faith predominates, religious identity is taken for granted and is rarely articulated in relation to other creeds. Islam, as the last of the great prophetic traditions beginning with Abraham, formally recognizes the prophets of Judaism and Christianity. Special relations are enjoined between Muslims, Christians, and Jews. Marriage is possible between Muslim men and Christian or Jewish women as *Ahl al-Kitāb* (People of the Book), and they are guaranteed special protection under the governance of a Muslim state.

There is evidence that minority Christian and Jewish communities, while residentially segregated, have coexisted in relatively peaceful conditions into the modern period. Despite the ravages of the Crusades, Christian communities did not experience communal violence against them in the religiously contested regions of the Near East, and Jewish communities in southwest Asia and North Africa did not experience the type of intercommunal violence that we associate with the anti-Semitic ghettos of eastern Europe or the pogroms of czarist Russia.[1] This is not intended to portray an unduly romantic picture of interreligious goodwill and social harmony among the three religious groups, but to express the idea that religious repression has not been a feature of early, medieval or modern Islam, in contrast to the religious oppression of Muslims and Jews in the Middle Ages in Europe, of which the Spanish Inquisition is the prime example.

Muslim-Christian Relations

Islam as a revealed tradition came only six centuries after the introduction of Christianity. As it began to spread, most dramatically in the seventh and eighth centuries of the common era, it replaced Christianity in many of the places where it had only recently secured a place. The attempt to reclaim Christianity and "lost" territory, especially the Holy Land, known as the Crusades, is a bitterly remembered chapter in Muslim-Christian history. The seizure and sacking of Jerusalem in 1099 by the *Faranj* ("French", or Crusaders) was an epic event in Muslim consciousness. The word *al-Faranj* is still used in colloquial Arabic to refer to a foreigner and Westerner. In Arabic the distinction is made between the *Suq al-Arab*, the market where one buys locally made items, and the *Suq al-Faranji*, Western-style stores where one buys appliances and other Western-produced items.[2]

Added to this early and highly negative episode in Christian-Muslim history is the era of European colonialism, which introduced a new element of the power of European Christianity allied with local indigenous Christian groups. With Islamic institutions either isolated or co-opted by colonialism, local Christian communities were strategically placed to work with colonial officials and to benefit more than Muslim communities, relatively speaking, from the presence of colonialism. The proselytization of Western culture and values through Christianity and the use of missionaries encouraged by colonial governments was not opposed by the Christian communities, although their presence was perceived as undue interference in religious affairs by local Muslim communities.

As a result, the nationalist movements carried with them a certain sentiment regarding the restoration of Islam and by extrapolation, the diminished influence of Christianity. Because many nationalist leaders saw the divisive role that religion played in this context, they rejected a political role for religion in the new postindependence states. However, others pressed for an Islamic model of government. In the immediate postcolonial period, Arab nationalism and secularism won the day and popular nationalist leaders were both Christian and Muslim. Decades later, with few political or economic advances made by secularist politics, the Islamist model is gaining ground. This is certainly perceived as a threat to Arab-Christian communities. For example, in the southern Sudan, where chronic civil war has ravaged the countryside and resulted in the deaths or dislocation of millions of people, rebel forces define themsleves as Christian and animist, waging their struggle against northern Muslim domination and Islamic fundamentalism.

Christian minority groups exist in significant numbers in Egypt, where the Coptic minority is 10 percent of the population; in Syria and Iraq, with 13 percent and 4 percent minorities, respectively; in the Sudan, with a 30 percent Christian and animist minority; and in Lebanon, where Maronite and Eastern Rite Christians represent almost half of the nation's population. These communities, including the nonminority Lebanese case, exist in relatively encapsulated groups, sharing common residential areas and socializing and marrying within the local group. In most ways their patterns of extended family life and endogamous marriage mirror their Muslim counterparts in each nation. Some Christian families have specialized in an area of manufacturing or trade, such as goldworking or Oriental carpet sales, and have developed prosperous livelihoods within a predominantly Muslim marketplace. Others have remained quite poor, like their fellow Muslim citizens in the relatively poorer nations, such as Egypt and the Sudan.

In Egypt, Copts are among the most influential national families, such as the family of the current head of the United Nations, Boutros Boutros

Ghali, and they are among the poorest of city dwellers, as they are disproportionately represented among the *Zabaleen* or garbage collectors. This is partly explained by the Muslim prohibition on the eating of pork; in response Copts have tended to monopolize pig production and butchering in Egypt and use the substantial Cairene garbage heaps to "graze" their pigs. This lowly occupation nonetheless can be quite lucrative, but does reinforce Muslim ideas about the uncleanliness of pigs and their association with Christians.

Depending on the government in power, the Coptic church and its leaders and institutions have been subjected to religious control and repression. The Coptic patriarch, Pope Shenouda, has often been under house arrest for speaking out against the government and its lack of representation of Copts and their interests. The current wave of Islamic revival in Egypt has had a negative impact on the Coptic community, especially in the central Egyptian town of Assiut, which is a center both of Coptic concentration and of militant Islamist activity. A number of armed attacks against Copts has alarmed the Christian community and has been staunchly opposed by the Egyptian government. Less-violent assaults on the culture of Coptic Christianity have occurred in metropolitan Cairo, where the popular Christmas displays in the stores downtown have been curtailed due to Islamist pressure. Accounts of repeated apparitions of the Virgin Mary in a Coptic neighborhood in Cairo during the 1980s were popularly accepted by Muslim and Christian Egyptians alike as a sign or warning to adopt a more religious path in social governance.

In the Sudan Christian leaders and communicants are identified with the southern resistance to northern dominance, most recently being perpetrated by an Islamist regime. In this country, Christianity is on the rise primarily as a reaction to intensified political Islamization (see Fluehr-Lobban, 1990). The fundamental problems are those of national unity, uneven economic development, and fair representation of the nation's multiple regions and ethnic groups, but the battleground rhetoric is religious, with Christians pitted against Muslims. Even before the Islamists came to power in 1989, the presence of Christian missionaries in the southern region was viewed as an example of neocolonialism, with a continuation of undue influence and interference from the West. Various governments from independence in 1956 to the present have engaged in the political expulsion of missionaries as agents of foreign governments and Western culture. Similar Christian-Muslim tensions exist in Chad and in Nigeria.

Muslim-Jewish Relations

The generally harmonious and collaborative relationship between Jewish and Muslim people can be documented within the classical histories of each community. As "protected" people (*dhimmis*) under the various Muslim caliphates, such as the Ummayads in Spain, Christian and Jewish communities enjoyed security and tolerance. Although they paid a tax (*jizya*) required of all non-Muslims and their religious practice could not openly compete with the Islamic faith (Hourani 1991: 117), Christians and Jews held a number of important bureaucratic and governmental positions, and Jewish scholars compiled the books of the Talmud in Baghdad under Abbasid protection. Jewish and Muslim scholars of the Middle Ages were responsible for the translation of the great Arabic works of science and philosophy from antiquity and for introducing them to Europe. Under Ottoman rule, Jewish communities were ruled autonomously under the Millet system of government. This continued until the fall of the Ottoman Empire after the end of World War I.

The status of Jewish communities in Arab-Islamic societies grew more complicated after the creation of the state of Israel in 1948. Prior to this important date, so-called Sephardic (or Middle Eastern Jewish communities) were scattered throughout the Maghrib in North Africa and in the Arabian Peninsula and southwest Asia. The term *Sephardic,* meaning originating in Spain, excludes the long established Jewish communities that had no historical relationship to Spain or to the expulsion of Jews after 1492 (Eickelman 1989: 329). Some diaspora communities have existed for a long time, such as the community at al-Ghriba on the Isle of Jerba in Tunisia, which has existed at least from the time of the fall of Jerusalem in 70 C.E.

Jewish communities lived in relative peace in dominantly Muslim areas until 1948, when many Sephardic Jews joined European Ashkenazi Jews in the newly created state of Israel. The war fought over the future of Palestine was a bitter one between the Zionists and Palestinians, but the Arab-Muslim world had no decisive political response since most of the region was still under European control. Many Middle Eastern Jews elected to remain within the countries of their birth and ancestors, and nonhostile relations between Muslims and Jews continued until the humiliating defeat of Arab-Muslim armies in the 1967 war with Israel. This blow to Arab-Muslim pride and, ultimately, to Arab nationalism produced an emotional and subjective reaction against local Jewish communities, and most left for Israel or the West.

Subsequent international politics of the Arab-Israeli conflict, involving East-West tensions and regional alignments, not to mention chronic outbreaks of war and conflict, have exacerbated subjective feelings on all sides. Few, however, would argue that the conflict is about religion, and it can be predicted that a successful negotiated resolution of the issues will bring about a resumption of the relations between Muslims and Jewish people that prevailed before 1948 and 1967. The future of Jerusalem, a city sacred to the Judaic, Christian, and Islamic faiths, as an open, accessible shrine to the faithful of the Abrahamic tradition is crucial to the restoration of goodwill and neighborly relations among Muslims, Christians and Jews.

Ethnic Identity: Who Is an Arab?

The ethnic diversity found in Middle Eastern and Islamic society is obscured by simple stereotypes regarding Arabs and a basic ignorance of the cultural and linguistic geography of the region. Iranians (Persians) are not Arabs, and although they employ Arabic calligraphy in the writing of their language, Farsi is an Indo-European and not a Semitic language. Likewise, the Turks, whom we associate with pre-twentieth century imperial rule of the region through the Ottoman Empire, are not Arabs. Before the modern reforms of Mustafa Kemal Atatürk in the 1920s, they too wrote their Central Asian language using Arabic calligraphy. Today in the Islamic Republic of Pakistan, Urdu is also written in Arabic calligraphy, emphasizing Pakistani Islamic religious identity over their ethno-linguistic roots.

Arab is an elusive ethnic, cultural and linguistic term—it has even been used as a racial designation. Ethnologically, an Arab is one who traces descent to the Arab tribes (lineages) of the Arabian Peninsula. This would be simple enough were it not for the explosive and dramatic spread of Islam by the Arabs during the first century after the introduction of Islam in Arabia in the seventh century of the common era. Given that great historical expansion and migration of people through the first *jihāds* in southwest Asia (contemporary Iraq, Iran, and Syria-Palestine)

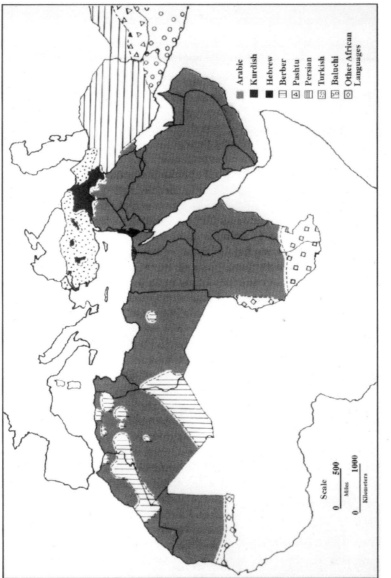

Legend:

Arabic
Kurdish
Hebrew
Berber
Pashtu
Persian
Turkish
Baluchi
Other African
Languages

Scale

0   500
    Miles
0   1000
    Kilometers

Fig. 4. Middle Eastern languages. From *The Middle East: An Anthropological Approach* by Dale F. Eickelman, p. 13. Copyright 1989. Reprinted by permission of Prentice-Hall, Inc., Englewood Cliffs, NJ 07632.

and North Africa from Egypt to Morocco to southern Europe, Arabs settled and mingled with local populations and forged a new Arab-Muslim identity in these areas over the succeeding centuries. Tracing descent through Arab lineages, especially through that of the Prophet, the *Quraysh,* has always been favored and, perhaps, amplified beyond actual genealogy and is therefore probably more fictive than real.

This blending of people and cultures through the spread of Islam has fostered the development of indigenous concepts, such as "Afro-Arab" identity, which was spawned in the context of the Sudanese nationalist movement. This was intended to solve the problem of having to identify exclusively with either African or Arab nations and cultures at the time of independence, and it flourished more as a political than as a cultural concept.

The precise definition of who is an Arab is elusive, but the sociological definition is more easily derived if we adopt a methodology of simply asking people if they identify themselves as Arabs. The question is simple but the answer is not. People who speak Arabic as a first language are likely to identify themselves as Arabs. However, the term 'Arab in the Arabic language has multiple meanings and derivations, and depending upon one's social background and place in society may evoke different responses.

Purely speaking, the term 'Arab refers to nomads, Bedouin, or people who move about, using animal husbandry as the major economic adaptation.[3] Being nomads and living in deserts or at the peripheries of settled, domesticated townspeople or urban dwellers, Arab nomads are not thought of as civilized in the ways that the more dominant agrarian or urban people see themselves. To be an Arab in this sense is to be somewhat uncouth or living wild in a state of nature. Indeed, there is a historical antipathy between nomads and settled agriculturalists, evidenced in their conflicts over scarce resources, such as water and grazing lands. So one may readily hear disparaging references made to Arabs when the reference is to Bedouin or desert dwellers.

The most significant twentieth century context of the use of the term Arab is in association with the political movement of Arab nationalism, articulated by many nationalist leaders in anticolonial movements throughout the Middle East and given international recognition and regional meaning by Gamal Abdel Nasser. Nasser became the symbolic leader of Arab nationalism in the mid-1950s when Egypt nationalized the Suez

Canal and Nasser stood up to the imperial pressure of Britain and France, allied with Israel, and succeeded in achieving Egyptian control over the canal. Dean Acheson, then U.S. secretary of state, sided with Egypt at a critical moment and helped to avoid all-out war over the Suez "crisis." Motivated by Arab nationalism, Nasser forged a short-lived union with Syria, known as the United Arab Republic (U.A.R.). Long after Syria withdrew from this union, Egypt continued to refer to itself as the U.A.R. Nasser was revered throughout the Arabic-speaking world as a great leader of the Arabs and people proudly identified themselves as Arabs.

After Nasser's death in 1969, the leadership of the Arab nationalist movement was unclear and various spokesmen of this political philosophy took their turn, including Muammar Qaddafi of Libya, Yasir Arafat of the Palestine Liberation Organization, and the Ba'thist leaders Hafez Asad in Syria and Saddam Hussein in Iraq. The political appeal to the so-called Arab Nation made by these and other leaders proved to be powerful rhetoric, if not powerful politics. The first great blow to Arab nationalism came in the 1967 Six Day War, in which Israel invaded and seized territory from three separate Arab nations—Egypt, Jordan and Syria—without a concerted military response from the Arab Nation. This war was a humiliating defeat to the Arab nations and the beginning of a popular skepticism of their leaders. The latest, perhaps fatal, blow to Arab nationalism came during the Gulf War of 1991, when the Arab nations of Kuwait and Saudi Arabia were pitted against the Arab nation of Iraq and its allies.

Appeals to the Arab Nation continue to come from Palestinian nationalists, whose lack of a territorial base makes Arab nationalism a matter of essential politics. Some of the more eloquent spokesmen of Arab nationalism have been the Christian Palestinian leaders Naif Hawatmeh and George Habash. The juxtaposition of Arab and Israel in the usually hyphenated Arab-Israeli conflict adds to the sense of the Arabs being constituted as a single nation, although this amounts to a political chimera.

Arab nationalism has had a distinctly secular cast to its political rhetoric and practice, with religion either irrelevant, from the standpoint of politics, or kept separated from politics. Together with the rhetoric of the Arab Nation was the promise of democracy or the presentation of military regimes or single-party regimes as democratic. Failures of Arab solidarity, like the 1967 Six Day War or the 1991 Gulf War, have deeply undermined the political viability of Arab nationalism, as has the failure to economic security long promised by these regimes. While people may still respond emotionally to the call for Arab unity, the political dynamic is shifting away from Arab nationalism to Islamic revival.

So, perhaps the best definition of an Arab is someone who thinks of himself or herself as an Arab. This person speaks Arabic as a first language, but may be Christian or Muslim, and may or may not claim descent in the long genealogy of the Arabs and their historical relationship to Islam. This definition leaves out the vast majority of the world's Muslims, most of whom are not Arabs and do not live in the Middle East. There are also numerous Muslim but non-Arab ethnic groups in the Middle East as well as the three million non-Arab, non-Muslim Jewish people living in Israel.

Non-Arab, Muslim Ethnic Groups

There are numerous non-Arab ethnic groups in the Middle East that are frequently lumped with or confused with Arabs because they are part of nation-states in the Arab world. Some of the larger populations or better known examples include the Nubians of Egypt and Sudan; the Berbers of Morocco, Algeria and Tunisia; and the Kurds who occupy parts of two non-Arab states, Iran and Turkey, and one Arab nation, Iraq. Many people who identify with these ethnic groups also speak Arabic as a second language, especially if they are living in less isolated towns and cities, but they do not identify themselves as Arabs.

Nubians

The Nubians of Egypt and the Sudan present a study in contrasts, for their status as an ethnic minority differs dramatically between the two states. Nubians occupy regions in Egypt south of the first cataract at the city of Aswan, and in towns and villages along the Nile south to the Sudanese border and its major Nubian settlement from Wadi Halfa south to Dongola in northern Sudan. The unique civilization of Kush centered at Meroe ruled ancient Egypt for a time during the Twenty-fifth Dynasty and then developed its own unique culture, religion and written language. Kushites ruled ancient Nubia for another millennium between the fifth century B.C.E. and the fourth century C.E., when Nubia's kingdoms were Christianized. Nubia remained Christian for almost another millennium, until the penetration of Islamic influences in the thirteenth through the fifteenth centuries. (See Adams 1976 for a more comprehensive survey of this history.)

Historically Nubia acted as the corridor to Africa (although Egypt is sometimes forgotten as part of Africa). And from ancient Pharaonic times through the days of the Ottoman Turks and the British, Nubia was a place for slave taking; "Nubian" was even a generalized referent for slaves. The trade in Nubian slaves was primarily for the armies of the ancient Egyptians and later the Ottoman Empire, and for domestic labor. But Nubians were not enslaved as part of the Great Atlantic slave trade of the sixteenth to nineteenth centuries, which exploited West African slave markets. The legacy of slavery has lingered in the generally inferior status Nubians experience in Egypt, but it has not acted as a barrier to social advancement and influence in the Sudan.

In the Sudan Nubians and other northern, riverain peoples close to them, such as the Shayqiya and Ja'aliyin, were closely aligned with the English colonial administration and assumed many of the key government posts after independence. They have constituted, in effect, Sudan's ruling elite in marked contrast to the secondary status of Nubians to the north. Nubians in Egypt are called *Saeedis,* a rather neutral reference to their home in the southern part of the country, generally thought of as south of Assiut, but *Saeedi* also connotes rural, not urban, and a degree of cultural backwardness, darker skin color, and lower educational levels. This often translates into unskilled or semiskilled jobs when Nubians migrate to cities in the northern part of the country. By contrast, Nubians in Sudan move easily from their villages or towns in the north to professional positions in Khartoum in government, business, or the military without stigmatization. As a part of Sudan's ruling elite, they have been, in part, responsible for the inferior status imposed on southern Sudanese.

Nubians are united through language and custom and speak a group of related languages unrelated to Arabic known as Rotana, and various dialects such as Mahas and Kenuz-Dongolawi, which are spoken on either side of the Egyptian-Sudanese border (Fernea and Fernea 1991: 137). One of the distinctive features of Nubian history is the early conversion to Christianity of Nubian kingdoms, lasting until the fifteenth century. These kingdoms acted as a barrier to the penetration of

Islam into Nubia and further south until after their collapse. Nubian social organization was matrilineal until the penetration of Islamic influence, but even today there are remnants of matrilineal social organization that clearly contrast with Arab, strongly patrilineal traditions. One of these is the well-known Nubian pattern of postmarital residence with the bride's family until after the birth of the first child. Other remnant behaviors have been documented in a recent study of Nubian women (Jennings 1990) in which the role of women and matrilineal ties in the economics of marriage and the financial support of the couple has been demonstrated.

Nubia is also remembered in the West for the great disruption and relocation of people during the flooding of Nubia at the opening of the High Dam at Aswan. An international effort was mounted to save some of the antiquities in Nubia, and many sociological and anthropological studies were made of the process of removal and adjustment of Nubian peoples. Kom Ombo in Egypt and Khasm al-Girba in the Sudan became the well-known resettlement homes of the Nubians. The massive relocation of Nubian people in the early 1960s established a common sense of Nubian identity. Nubians travel freely between Egypt and the Sudan visiting relatives, but to do so they must traverse the great Lake Nasser, which was created by the Aswan High Dam, a powerful reminder of how their communities were forever changed by the demands of the nation-states of which they are part.

The Berbers

The Berbers are an ancient non-Arab people of northwest Africa occupying the interior and remote regions of what is today Tunisia, Algeria, and Morocco. As a Saharan people comprising a distinctive linguistic and cultural stock, they initially resisted Arab and Islamic penetration as they spread westward and south into the Maghrib. Being essentially nomadic, Arabs and Berbers shared a common lifestyle in adapting to a desert environment, but this is where the resemblance between Arab and Berber ends. Known for their fierce resistance to foreign intruders, the term *barbarian* is derived from the Greek encounter with the Berbers, whose language was non-Greek and therefore, in their perception, uncivilized. As the traditional inhabitants of the western Sahara they have controlled both desert and mountains, in the latter case seeking refuge as much as an economic niche. In part due to the foreign pressure

Berber village of Chinini in southern Tunisia. Berbers historically fled Roman and Arab invasions by retreating to mountainous areas.

to which they have been subjected, but also a result of their non-Arab ethnicity, the culture of hospitality with frequent visiting is generally not found among Berbers.

The Arab invasions began in the seventh century of the common era and the first century of Islam, and they first affected the indigenous regions along the Mediterranean coast. As the invasions continued during the next several centuries, Arabic language, culture, and the religion of Islam penetrated the interior of North Africa and spread among the local Berber peoples. The Berbers resisted this intrusion, having previously fled into mountainous regions to escape Greek and Roman domination, and Berbers only accepted Islam very gradually. Their matrilineal traditions also lacked compatibility with Arab patrilineal-patriarchal ones, and some of the important examples of resistance to Arab invasions were led by Berber warrior queens, known as *Kahenas*. When the Berbers did accept Islam, many did not follow the path of the religion of the ruling Arab dynasties, but accepted Kharijite ideas that permitted removal of an unpopular or unjust imām (Hourani 1991: 39), a practice more compatible to their egalitarian traditions. Some of the largest Berber confederations, such as the Sanhaja, were strong enough to resist altogether the Arab advance and the westernmost part of Africa remained outside of Arab control (Abu-Lughod 1980: 44).

Extensive linkages of new Arab empires crisscrossed the Sahara east from Egypt and the East, known as the Mashriq, to the Maghrib in the west of North Africa, while north and south trade routes connected the Mediterranean to the interior. In their path Berber culture gradually absorbed a generalized Arab-Islamic culture. Typically, this did not include fluency and literacy in Arabic or the great literary, scholastic traditions associated with this. Berber is a written language, known as Tifnac, and was a literate tradition carried mainly by women. It could not compete successfully with Arabic, however, and increasingly those Berbers who came within the sphere of urban life became Arabic speakers (Hourani 1991: 435). Outside of urban situations Berber dialects continue to be widely spoken in Algeria and Morocco, and even in parts of Tunisia, south of the historically important Arab-Islamic city of Kairouan.

A cultural and linguistic distinctiveness among Berbers has been maintained, with unique traditions maintained by large Berber groups in Morocco and Algeria, such as the Kabyle. Certain nomadic groups, such as the Tuareg of Morocco, have been made famous in the ethnographic literature by the custom of male veiling. Berbers maintained their language, local organization, leadership and sense of independence even during the era of French colonialism. Colonialism kept alive the divide between Arab and Berber, and in the case of colonial Morocco, Berber-speaking regions were formally removed from the jurisdiction of Islamic law, thus enforcing a policy of separation (Eickelman 1976: 256). The colonialists were thus surprised by the enthusiasm with which Berber peoples took up the nationalist struggle.

Much of their literature dealing with nationalist themes and Berber identity is written in French, since an educated Berber is likely to be more literate in French than in Arabic. The modern Arabic dialect spoken in the Maghrib is distinctive as well, and this is frequently attributed to the mixture of Berber and French words with Arabic vocabulary. Cultural encounters, like the one between Berbers and Arabs, and later with the French admixture, are rarely as clear as simple cultural domination by the invader. Resistance by the invaded to assimilation and the persistence of the subjugated group's ethnic identity is common, as the example of Berber culture shows.

The Kurds

Kurdistan, the homeland of the Kurdish people, is a region that stretches from the mountain ranges of the eastern Anatolian region in Turkey to northern Iraq and northwestern Iran. The Kurdish population of about 15 million people is another example of a substantial non-Arab group. Although the largest number of Kurds live in Turkey, their status was, until recently, politically unrecognized in that country. In the early 1990s the Turkish legislature abolished laws made at the time of the founding of the Turkish republic that made it illegal to speak Kurdish in public or to publish in the language. Kurds speak their indigenous language, Kurmanci, which is now recognized as a legitimate language for testimony in Turkish court. Recently a Kurdish Studies Institute has been established in Istanbul, helping to reverse the negative attitude of the Turkish government toward the Kurds.

The Kurds have not fared as well in Iran or Iraq. They have been historically repressed as a non-Arab minority in Iraq and as a non-Shī'a, non-Persian group in Iran. As members of the 'Alawi Islamic sect, they have been rejected by Sunni Muslims in Turkey and Iraq. Probably their status was better in the past when Kurdistan was administered autonomously under the Ottoman empire. The call for an independent Kurdistan or autonomous Kurdish regions within the states where they are found is likely to increase in the coming years.

The 'Alawi sect, to which most Kurds belong, is a branch of Islam that is marked by specialized religious practices that fall outside of the mainstream of both Sunni and Shī'a practice. For example, fasting takes place during twelve days of the month of Muharram as commemoration of the twelve imāms, and the fast is interpreted as a ritual of mourning for the martyrs at Karbala. Differences in prayer and in the performance of the faith associated with the major Islamic holidays, such as 'Id al-Kabīr, distinguish them as outsiders. Further, a secrecy and a reserve, no doubt stemming from historical persecution, has shrouded the 'Alawis in greater mystery.

During the 1991 Gulf War there were many news reports about the plight of the Kurds within Iraq, at risk because of their opposition to Saddam Hussein. This news story was the latest chapter in a history of tension between the Arab rulers of Iraq and the Kurdish ethnic minority in the northeast part of the country. As nomadic or semisedentary people at the periphery of the political center in Baghdad, they have been left out of the sweeping economic and social changes occurring in the nation. Kurdish nationalism has been a feature of "outsider" rule of the Kurds from the time of the Ottomans, through the period of the

British Mandate, and since the time of Iraqi independence in 1958. During times of tension between the nations where the Kurds are found, they have been subject to manipulation, as during the period of the Iran-Iraq war and the Gulf War. In Kurdish folklore a powerful theme represented is that the Kurds have no friends. At the moment there are few supranational calls for Kurdish independence. Perhaps as a part of the international response to end human rights abuses levied against the Kurds, the call for an independent Kurdistan will be heard some day.

Race: Its Utility as a Concept in Communal Identity

Anthropologists have abandoned the concept of "race" as misleading and lacking in scientific rigor. Race has been used to foster notions of purity, and it has been used to divide peoples purportedly not of the same racial stock. Human biologists and anthropolgists have experimented with racial classifications, and have generally found these to be hopelessly inadequate.

While scientific racial classification has all but disappeared, sociological categories based on group identity are nevertheless vital cultural and political constructs. The racial concept "black" means very little biologically or even phenotypically, but it conveys a great deal of political and cultural meaning in the United States. The American Bureau of Census and a host of business, professional, and educational institutions keep statistics on American racial groups, including categories such as "Black/African-American," "White/Caucasian," "Hispanic," "Native American," "Asian American," and "Other." Many Muslim peoples from the Middle East and North Africa have been confounded by these racial categories, and when asked to fill out these American forms, they have not known with which race they should identify. Some would say they they are African but not black; others report that they are frequently taken for being Hispanic and have been addressed in Spanish in American cities with large Hispanic populations; others, in frustration, might check "Other," since nothing else seems to fit. Some Affirmative Action guidelines have sought to clarify the question of race for North Africans and Middle Eastern persons by including these groups as "White/Caucasian".

Islamic society, with its broad geographic and cultural scope, is a multiracial grouping. This multiracial and multinational character of the

Umma is one of its most potent features. Because images of Allah, of the Prophet and his family, or any other form of idolatry are strictly forbidden in Islam, as Islam spread the convert did not have to accept a foreign image of God as "white" or any other picture of the deity in some human form. Allah, the supreme deity, as an abstraction, could be shaped in the mind of the convert.

There are numerous religious interpretations and historical studies that deal with the matter of race in Islam and Islamic society. The Qur'ān is replete with passages that reveal a nonracist view of humanity, where goodness is equated with righteous conduct and leading an upright Muslim life. Numerous Ḥadīth refer to humans being "like the teeth of a comb" with none superior to another save in the conduct of religion.

Notwithstanding religious preference for conversion to Islam and freedom from slave status, the practice of enslavement was present in Arab society at the time of the coming of Islam and has persisted into the twentieth century. Slavery was not legally abolished in Saudi Arabia until 1962. And the status of a "free" person or "slave" probably remains a significant category in such cases as the Rwala Bedouin society, where marriage between persons of slave and free origin is impossible or strongly stigmatized. Likewise in the Sudan, where slavery was officially abolished at the turn of the century, the slave status of persons remained a viable category well into the second half of the century. I recall vividly my own shock when a local district commissioner in southern Kordofan in 1971 presented to my husband and me an individual who was described as a slave among the Baggara people. Sadly, this recollection took on new meaning when Sudanese social scientists reported that slavery was revived among the Baggara and neighboring Rizeigat and Messiriya Arabs in the context of armed militia raids against southerners in the renewed civil war after 1983 (Mahmud and Baldo 1987).

There is a growing recognition that Islamic jurisprudence must stand decisively against any legacy of slavery that would adversely affect the rights of persons of alleged slave origin. In a landmark case in the Sudan in 1973, the Sharī'a High Court decided that a father's effort to block the marriage of his daughter to a man alleged to be the grandson of a slave was unfounded. The father had attempted to show that the proposed bridegroom and his family's background were not of equal status to his daughter and their family, an idea known as "equality of standard in marriage" (al-Kafa'a fil zawāj) in Islamic jurisprudence. After a lengthy appeals process, the High Court judges concluded that Islam recognizes the equality of all people and "There is no preference between an Arab and a non-Arab except by his God-fearing" (Fluehr-Lobban 1987: 127–129). This case and others like it ultimately resulted in changes in the personal status law in 1991 when pedigree or genealogy was removed as a condition restricting marriage.

On the other hand, slavery existed in the time of the Prophet, and it continued throughout the great Muslim empires and into the modern period. Middle Eastern slavery, mainly for domestic purposes, predated Islam and the new religion accepted this reality while recognizing certain legal rights of slaves in Muslim society. According to Islamic law, a free-born Muslim cannot be enslaved; slaves were taken from non-Muslim societies that were invaded or conquered. Slaves have the legal right to inherit property and conduct business, and such effects could result from a close master-slave relationship. Freeing a slave is recommended in the Qur'an as an act of contrition or expiation, and freed slaves can marry into the families of their former masters. Perhaps the best evidence for the Islamic approach to slavery—conversion to Islam and manumission—took place during the Mamluke dynasty, which ruled Egypt and Syria from the mid-thirteenth to early sixteenth centuries. The Mamlukes were military slaves—recruited as slave-soldiers from conquered lands in Central Asia, eastern Europe, and North Africa—who converted to Islam, were freed, and then came to rule. One of the most popular and widespread of stories from the Arabian Peninsula is that of Antar ibn Shaddad, the son of a slave woman, whose courage and adventures have been told and retold, probably since pre-Islamic times.

For better or worse, the institution of slavery was not challenged and rejected by Islam. Slaves could be elevated by deeds, religion, or knowledge, but they could also remain in servitude living with low status as social unequals. Many slaves were taken from the Sudan, Ethiopia, and Somalia. While some were ultimately incorporated into Arab society, others retained the stigmas attached to a social underclass. To a certain extent this correlates with race and phenotype. Dark-skinned Nubians, other Sudanese, and Africans may experience racial bigotry when they are traveling or working in countries where the legacy of slavery is still apparent, such as in the Arab Gulf countries. The referent 'Abīd (slave) has both a racial and class dimension. The term Zinjī is also used to refer to "blacks", non-Arab Africans, or African-Americans, and while it carries descriptive and sometimes pejorative meaning, it lacks the specific stigma of slavery.

The Legacy of Slavery in Sudan

Slavery in nineteenth century southern Sudan was a time, according to Dinka writer Francis Deng, when "the world was spoiled." The warfare, raiding, and capture of humans by soldiers in the Turco-Egyptian army was justified by the fact that the ethnic groups in the south of Sudan were not Muslims, and were, therefore, fair game. The British, who emerged from four centuries of involvement in the Atlantic slave trade as champions of an antislavery campaign, encouraged the idea that Islam sanctioned the trade. They used this as part of a Christian crusade to rid the Sudan of Islamic rule under the Mahdī in the late nineteenth century. Indeed, efforts by the Mahdī to bring areas of the south under Islamic control are remembered by southerners as an encounter filled with bitterness and fear of Arabs and Muslims.

The British established control over the Sudan in 1898, and during the decades of colonialism until independence in 1956, the south was administered separately from the north, while the linguistic, cultural, and religious divide between them widened. Christian missionaries were sent into the south by the colonial government to provide basic education and health services. Prejudice against southerners as non-Muslims was compounded by attitudes of cultural and racial inferiority. Phenotypically distinct, the southerners were ready targets for racist referents, most typically and painfully the term 'abīd (slave). The south as a region was basically left out of the first postindependence government, and successive northern governments attempted to solve the "southern problem" through an imposed Islamization. Resistance to this solution has led to a chronic state of civil war between the Muslim north and the animist and Christian south. This is a cruel legacy of slavery with a strong racialist cast to it that must be confronted directly and resolved before Sudanese unity is achieved.

A Semitic Race?

The designations Semite and Semitic have been used to describe the Arab and Jewish peoples. In Euro-American history and culture, Semite has been applied to the Jewish presence in Western society, so that the negative referent "anti-Semitic" has been used almost exclusively to mean bigotry or racism as applied to Jewish people. Anti-Arab prejudice has witnessed an alarming increase in the West in the past several decades and can justifiably be included as another unfortunate form of anti-Semitism.

The Semites are an ancient people tracing their common linguistic heritage to Mesopotamia about 2500 B.C.E. The "sons of Shem", Semites diverged into distinctive language and cultural groups that included the Arabs and Hebrews—the legendary descendants of the sons of Abraham, Ismail and Isaac—and also people speaking related Semitic languages, such as Aramaic and Amharic. According to some linguists Semites living in the Sinai took the Egyptian syllabary and converted it into the first true alphabet in which a sign or letter represented a single sound. Thus only a few dozen characters had to be memorized, and in this way literacy became accessible to ordinary people instead of a monopoly controlled by priests and scribes. The Hebrews also perfected monotheism and originated the idea of the single, unchallenged deity through the prophet Abraham, who is revered as progenitor to all of the Abrahamic faiths—Judaism, Christianity and Islam (Peters 1982).

The Hebrews were already a distinctive people at the time of Babylonian captivity, and in the tenth century B.C.E. when the Hebrew territories of Judea and Samaria were united into the kingdom of Israel under King David. This kingdom was short-lived, and after only a century of existence, a dispersal of the Hebrew peoples took place into parts of southwest Asia, North Africa, the Iberian Peninsula, and other parts of Europe.

The Arabs settled and flourished in al-Jazīra al-Arabīyya, literally the "island of the Arabs", the Arabian Peninsula. The northern Arabs were nomadic camel-herders or oasis dwellers, and the southern Arabs developed commercial centers and urban life. Situated strategically along the trade routes of the Red Sea, Arabian Sea, and Indian Ocean the island of the Arabs was a natural crossroads in the east-west trade between the Mediterranean and the Indian Ocean. Into this context of international trade and commerce in the Arabian Peninsula, Islam was introduced, grounded in Arab culture but knowledgeable of the world outside Arabia. With the introduction of Islam the Abrahamic tradition of prophecy was complete, as was the divergence of the original Semites into distinctive religious and cultural communities.

After the great expansion of Islam in the first centuries after its introduction, when the caliphates were established in Baghdad, Damascus, and Andalusia in Spain, Jewish and Christian residents of these areas were officially protected as *dhimmis,* or "People of the Book". Jewish scholarship flourished, and while the communities remained separate, there is no evidence of intercommunal violence or systematic discrimination that we might call racism today. Indeed, there is every indication that the reason for the flowering of Andalusia was its multilingual, multicultural, and multireligious character. Scholars carried out their research and writing in Arabic, Latin, and Hebrew, and ordinary people spoke an Andalusian dialect of Arabic and the Romance dialect that developed into Spanish (Hourani 1991: 194). In 1492, with the ascendance of a Christian monarchy in Spain, both the Muslims (Moors) and the Jews were expelled and victimized in the infamous Spanish Inquisition. The Sephardic Jews, those fleeing from Spain to North Africa and parts of the Middle East, resettled with Arab-Muslim communities with whom they were already familiar. Again, no pattern of intercommunal, interreligious conflict is recorded, although no significant blending of the communities through intermarriage took place.

The experience of Jewish people in Europe and Russia, the Ashkenazim, was quite different. The religious blame placed on the Jews for the killing of Christ and the isolation of Jewish communities in reaction made them an easy target for religious and racial harassment, documented in the case of urban Jews in the ghettos of major European cities and the systematic pogroms of rural and urban Jews in czarist Russia. This historical context gave rise in Europe to the nineteenth century Jewish nationalist movement, called Zionism, not in any Arab or Muslim capital where Jewish people historically resided. The fulfillment of Zionist aspirations after the end of World War II, with the creation of the state of Israel and the displacement of Palestinian Arab people, has altered the preexisting relationship between Arab-Muslim and Jewish peoples.

An enmity engendered by politics has replaced the traditional tolerance between the religious-cultural groups. But I do not believe that it is racial at its core. Over the years I have heard many angry comments about Israeli politics from Muslim and Arab friends, but I have not heard the kind of anti-Semitic remarks and stereotypes that are common in the United States. This gives me a sense of optimism that a negotiated peace between Israel and its Arab neighbors will bring about a restoration of Arab-Muslim and Jewish relations as they once were, the essentials of this being tolerance, mutual respect, and peaceful coexistence.

Is there a Semitic race? Race, as defined by anthropologists and biologists as a people breeding in relative isolation for extended periods of time, is a term that does not apply to either Arab or Jewish people, whose antiquity and influence over a great expanse of time and geography has been the antithesis of isolation. Semites, both Arabs and Jews, share a common ancient heritage and shared history after the advent of Islam.

Class and Economics in Ideology and Practice

While Islamic and Arab society are egalitarian in fundamental ideology of religion and family and community life, hierarchical differences have been clearly in evidence since the earliest days of state and empire. Travel to any major metropolis in the Middle East reveals great discrepancies between rich and poor, even observed at the most superficial level. Egyptian Nobel Laureate Neguib Mahfouz brought international attention to the conditions of urban life in Cairo, especially in his classic *Midaq Alley*. The maintenance of the egalitarian ethos, like the myth of democracy in America, is a powerful ideology that can be drawn upon to mobilize masses of people and to shape everyday interactions. But the historical record is filled with evidence that class differences have been pronounced and felt in every aspect of especially urban but also rural life.

Large urban-based families engaged in local and international commerce comprised the nascent bourgeoisie of the medieval Muslim state. Great land-owning feudal lords, often known as *pashas* owing to their heyday in the Ottoman Empire, governed every aspect of the economy and society of the peasants they controlled. They became powerful as well as rich and used the traditional ideology of nasab to suggest a genealogical connection to their rule and influence. The European powers were only too happy to use these indigenous notables to assist in their own economic and political control of their colonies. With independence these powerful families were only partly diminished by land reforms and government regulations that followed popular control of national resources. In Egypt and other countries that underwent significant land reform the reformer, Gamal Abdel Nasser, became a hero to the peasants. However, in other cases, such as the Sudan, the notables themselves came to power and nationalized the apparatus of government without altering the traditional centers of power and wealth.

The development of the oil industry in countries of the Arabian peninsula and the Persian Gulf has expanded the economic gap with the non-oil-producing countries, which have become labor-exporting countries. During the past two decades of opening up of the economies to largely unregulated Western investment, what the Egyptians call *infitāh*, the gap between rich and poor within nations has become as dramatic as the gap between rich and poor states in the Middle East. The factor of class difference has become more evident as the focus has shifted from outside economic control to domestic class differentiation.

The major modern economic contradiction in the Arab Middle East has been the extraordinary wealth generated by the oil-producing countries and the inability of dominantly agrarian economies elsewhere to compete. In response, these capital-poor countries have devised economic strategies that were supposed to open up local economies to compensate for being left out of the oil boom. Egypt, the Sudan, Jordan, Syria, former North Yemen, and Tunisia have all followed economic policies that can be considered infitāh. These policies have included measures that relax controls over the economy to facilitate the entrance of foreign, typically Western capital, the productive investment of domestic capital, and the export of domestic labor to the oil-producing or former colonial countries (Kerr and Yassin 1982: 4). The results have been less than dramatic, for the loosely regulated foreign investments tend to stifle rather than stimulate indigenous capital. Thus the economic growth is largely foreign and extractive rather than of the type which develops an infrastructure and lays the base for long-term, sustainable development.

Domestic labor is not mobilized for long-term projects and is valuable primarily because it is cheap. However, with the rising costs of commodities due to the artificial injection of wealth into the local economy and emphasis on consumer items, poorly paid local workers can no longer afford the high cost of living in their own countries. So domestic skilled laborers must migrate elsewhere for employment, usually to the Arabian Peninsula or to oil-rich countries of the Persian Gulf. In turn, the domestic economy becomes increasingly dependent on the remittances of workers abroad. During the economic boom of the 1980s in oil production, the economies of poorer countries were buoyed by these workers' remittances; in Egypt they accounted for about one-fifth of GNP. But with the economic downturn of the latter part of the decade and into the

1990s, local economies have suffered both the return of workers who are not easily absorbed into the domestic economy and the loss of their remittances.

Effects of Large-Scale Labor Migration

The ripple effect of this regional imbalance between capital-producing and labor-exporting nations is felt in virtually every city, town, and village in the region. The oil-rich countries, with acute labor shortages for their expanding economies, are able to employ schoolteachers and university professors, as well as domestics, car drivers, and other service personnel from all over the Arab and Islamic world. Saudi Arabia's working class is mostly foreign, including large numbers of Yemenis, Egyptians, Sudanese, and Muslim workers from non-Arab countries such as Malaysia and Pakistan. Emigration to Saudi Arabia, Kuwait, or other oil rich countries, in the sense of long term residence and eventual citizenship, is out of the question due to tight regulation of foreign workers.

The outflow of semiskilled and skilled labor from the poorer Muslim and Arab countries usually means the loss of that nation's youngest and most productive workers. The initial drain came from the cities of the poorer countries, but eventually a continuous process of rural to urban labor migration within the country was carried forward to its logical extension. Towns and villages have been drained of agricultural workers, and many villages have been all but abandoned to women, the very old, and the very young. There is even a slight increase in the number of women workers migrating from the rural areas to the city and then to the labor importing countries, even though culturally this is risky and unacceptable.

Some young men intend to work abroad only long enough to earn enough money to marry and settle down at home. However, the ever-weakening local economies cannot reabsorb workers accustomed to higher wages and certain levels of food and commodity consumption. Married men working outside of their countries are nevertheless still responsible for the support of their families, according to Islamic law, and those who fail to do so may find a case raised against them by their wives. There has been a sharp increase in non-support cases during this period of massive expatriate labor migration. The Shari'a courts, with a high responsibility to the Umma world community of Muslims, cooperate internationally to litigate such cases. A summons can be issued in

Cairo or Khartoum and received in Jidda where it is delivered to the accused party.

Arab Development Banks and Islamic Development Programs

A number of solutions to this regional economic imbalance have been proposed, involving Western technology, Arab or Muslim capital, and indigenous labor. The potential partnership for purposes of economic development of Western technology purchased by Arab capital and managed by local labor has been more attractive in theory than in practice. Western technological ventures have been more interested in contract work than in a long-term commitment to a development project, while Arab capital has been unwilling to risk a venture that may not be profitable without the commitment of time necessary to successful completion of a project (Salacuse 1982: 132).

Various Arab development funds, such as the Kuwait Fund for Arab Economic Development and the Arab Monetary Fund (founded in 1961 and 1976, respectively), have been organized for several decades on the principle that surplus Arab capital, generated in the oil-producing countries with their relatively small populations and limited agricultural resources, should be invested in the capital-poor nations with large labor pools and greater agricultural potential. The Sudan and Egypt were considered prime targets for financing of such Arab development projects. In fact, the flow of Arab capital into these poorer nations has been relatively timid, due to politically generated risks of failure and elevated expectations of the recipient nations. Some agreements were rejected because they involved small interest payments on loans (at 4 percent compared with higher Western interest rates) on the grounds that no interest should be charged between Arab "brothers" (Salacuse 1982: 144). Nationalistic considerations came into play when foreign investors, Arab and non-Arab, sought to buy into safer ventures, such as real estate. The potential sale of precious land near to the pyramids at Giza by a Japanese investor for the purpose of a golf course and tourist resort galvanized the Egyptian nation and served to symbolize the plight of a poor country desperately seeking foreign capital.

The common bond of Islam between capital-rich and capital-deficit nations in the region has engendered a religiously based system of financing and investment, with the creation of the Islamic Development Bank in 1974 and private Islamic banks, such as the Faisal Islamic Bank, both using Saudi capital. Another financial group employing Islamic principles is the Baraka Group of Bahrain. Conforming to the Islamic principle of a ban on usury (*riba*), usually interpreted as any form of direct interest charges, these financial groups and development banks employ the investment alternative of shared ventures, where the capital is provided by one partner and the labor and management of the project are provided by the other partner. Together they share the risks and profits in proportions agreed upon in advance of the undertaking.

As a religiously based alternative for economic investment, there is much to be admired in Islamic investment. With their philosophy of sharing of capital and labor, risk and profit, they have helped to mobilize indigenous small businesses that had been alienated and rejected by the power of traditional wealth concentrated in the hands of a few families. However, the Islamic banks have also acted as a funnel for controlled investment, as in the financing of Islamist groupings, such as the National Islamic Front in the Sudan, which has pursued a political agenda of Islamization against the rational economic interests of the nation as a whole. It is ironic that the religiously correct Islamic banks and financial groups operate primarily outside of the Arabian Peninsula, while the major Western banks are favored within these oil-producing countries.

Relations with Foreigners: Focus on Westerners

There are a number of indigenous categories in Islam and Arab society that reflect conceptions about "the other," in this case especially the Western outsider. There are, of course, numerous examples of how Sudanese conceptualize Egyptians and vice versa; how Saudis view Malaysian Muslims, and so forth, but since the intended audience for this work is Western and American, the focus is on views of Westerners.

The main word for foreigner, meaning Westerner, is *al-Gharīb*, coming from the root meaning "from the West," but also connoting that which is strange or foreign. The term could be compared favorably to our use of "the East", the Orient, to mean the strange and exotic. *Al-Ajnabi* is also used to mean foreigner in modern standard Arabic. Referents that stem directly from colonial contact include *khawāja*, probably begun in Ottoman Turkish times to indicate a foreign ruler or person of wealth and power, and carried forward into European colonial times with similar meaning. Also the term *Faranji* was applied to the French foreign colonial and commercial presence in the Levant.

All of these terms are in active use in the Arab world today, and each has its own distinctive secular historical context. From the point of view of Islam, the world is traditionally divided into Muslim and non-Muslim, historically the *Dār al-Islām* (the abode of peace) and *Dār al-Harb* (the place of war). In the early centuries of Islam as it was spreading more through conquest than by trade, this was an accurate division of the world. But decades of Western colonial rule have placed most Islamic societies in a defensive position, where the struggle is to maintain the essentials of Islam in the face of foreign rule and economic control. The contemporary jihadist call to regain Islamic ascendancy recalls some of this division of the world into the place of Islam and peace and the place of war.

Vigorous nationalist movements were witnessed in every British and French colony, but soon after independence the local politicians and merchants almost invariably welcomed foreigners' return as guests in the new nations. Americans, lacking the particular history of a colonial relationship, nevertheless have been treated more or less in the same category as former colonialists and therefore as powerful foreigners. As the United States assumed the leadership of the West after World War II, the power or motive of some individual Americans may have been misinterpreted. When Richard and I first went to the Sudan and embarked upon a program of language learning and life among people, some acquaintances joked that the CIA was becoming even more sophisticated, sending nice young Americans to learn colloquial Arabic in order to be better spies on the people.

While Americans and Europeans are not culturally distinguished except by the more cosmopolitan sectors of society, African-Americans have a different experience than Euro-Americans. They are often taken for being North African, or Arab, and they may be approached as a fellow countryperson, until the first impression is corrected. Many Arabs and Africans are interested in the historical experience and contemporary status of African-Americans in the United States and may include black Americans with other third world peoples, but in nearly every case African-Americans are distinguished from other Americans.

Westerners may be thought of in stereotypical ways, as we in the West tend to stereotype Muslims and Arabs. Western life is generalized as being of high standard, and the idea of poor people in these wealthy countries may be challenging to communicate. Whiskey drinking is thought to be common for Western men (perhaps a holdover from colonial times), while Western women may be considered to be of looser morals, like the women portrayed in Hollywood films. Both sexes are seen as living the good life, preferring nightclubs to more serious activities. The Wild West image has taken root whereby American society is thought to be violent and dangerous.

With sexuality generally less regulated and sex easily accessible, Western society is conceived of as somewhat decadent. Women's relatively greater freedom is not necessarily envied. Within an Islamic framework Western women are seen as unprotected and therefore open prey for sexual exploitation. The Western family is a particular target for Islamist propaganda that exhorts Muslim activists not to mimic Western values. The high rate of divorce in the West and the growing number of single-parent families, usually headed by women, are viewed as examples of women's vulnerable condition. In addition the drug problem and the prevalence of AIDS and other sexually transmitted diseases are well publicized and the conclusion often reached is that Western society is out of control. It is with fear and trepidation that sons are sent to the West to study, and daughters are rarely permitted to study abroad.

Western education, however, is admired. Young men and, to a lesser extent, women may leave their countries to study in the technical areas, for the technological advancement of the West is much admired. Students are encouraged to study the physical and biological sciences, engineering, medicine, and computer technology in Europe and the United States. It is hoped that they will return home to utilize these skills in the development and welfare of their countries. This is not always the case, for the temptations of the West are powerful, in terms of a comfortable material life free from the traditional responsibilities to the extended family. Some young men stay for an extended period of time to complete their studies; they enjoy the relatively greater freedom possible in the West, but then return home to marry. Others marry in the West, and have to confront cultural and religious differences in order to sustain the relationship.

Apart from the unusual contact with visitors, like anthropologists or other academics who have come to stay for extended visits, most foreigners fall into the category of either tourists or professionals and diplomats conducting business in the Muslim areas of the Middle East.

The tourists are readily identifiable by their national costume and travel gear. In most places and situations they are welcomed with traditional Arab hospitality. There are a few exceptions to this general rule. Visits to the interior of mosques are generally not permitted in the Maghrib and have been curtailed in places where Islamist activism has been a feature of local politics, but such visits are entirely permissible in Egypt and Turkey where some of the most beautiful examples of Islamic architecture are found. The normal hospitality found throughout the region is also compromised by the European custom of nude sunbathing and swimming found commonly throughout the northern rim of the Mediterranean, but not acceptable in the Muslim southern Mediterranean. Some Europeans, apparently oblivious to the fact that they are visiting a Muslim country, will visit the southern Mediterranean public beaches and dress (or undress) as though they were visiting the Cote d'Azure. In Tunisia, which boasts some of the most beautiful beaches and where tourism is officially encouraged, many Muslims who are offended by open nudity blame their government rather than the visitors for permitting the practice. Lacking this custom at home, Americans are not guilty of this cultural offense, but they are also less likely to travel to these areas simply for the beaches.

Of the Western professionals resident or visiting the region, there is likely to be more contact with the businessman than the diplomat, whose range of public activities is somewhat circumscribed. It is the unusual diplomat or spouse who involves himself or herself with the social life of the host country, but those who do so are much admired. American diplomats trained for work in Arab-Muslim countries in recent years have been better prepared in language and cultural areas, so that public events, such as might be sponsored by the American Cultural Center, can be conducted in the Arabic language.

The Western journalist or businessperson who lacks sufficient language training must interact using English in order to conduct business. To do so effectively, they need to become culturally sensitive to develop their relationships. Men interact best with other men, and should expect evening engagements not to include the wife of the colleague, unless the invitation is to the man's home. Even at home, in more conservative contexts, the wife may make only a perfunctory appearance, or none at all. Western women, as business representatives or journalists, do their best interviewing or conduct of business with other women. However, it is likely that their local contacts are men. Avoiding nighttime appointments reduces the ambiguity of Western–Middle Eastern male-female relations.

Recalling Arab and Islamic values of hospitality and generosity, it is imperative that the host pays the bill, for example after a restaurant dinner meeting. You may have to insist several times and persist with open evidence of intent to pay, such as cash or credit card, but you must be successful, for to allow your guest to pay is shameful. Likewise, the Westerner must permit the Arab-Muslim host to display his generosity when you are the guest; Dutch treat arrangements are inappropriate and are a Western solution to this awkward problem. Multiple meetings may also be necessary in order to accomplish the task at hand, so the Westerner should gauge the length of stay accordingly. Also, typically, the work day ends sooner than in the West, so mornings are better than afternoons. Arab and Muslim etiquette prevents a person from saying no directly, so picking up on nuance of meaning is important, even when the language of communication is English. Unsophisticated Westerners may interpret the indirect no as slyness or the possibility of a deferred decision, but in this case usually persistence will not pay off.

Western notions of time and of being on time may have to be adjusted in order to allay frustration. Arab and Middle Eastern society moves at a slower, more socially inclusive pace. One is never in such a hurry that there is no time to stop and chat with a neighbor or associate. Also, telephones, public transportation and other means of communication and getting about may not be as efficient as the Westerner expects, so patience is also an asset. Allowing a half-hour or more to the appointed time may still be within a local definition of being on time, so the experienced Westerner may add this amount of time to an appointment and arrive just as his or her guest arrives. As a more relaxed relationship develops, different concepts of time can be discussed and joked about, such as "Is that 10 o'clock Western or Eastern time?" The Sudanese refer to Western time as appearing on the hour, *Ala shoka,* meaning, "as on the prong of the fork."

Notes

1. Anti-Semitism, referring to anti-Jewish sentiment as it has been known in Europe, is used awkwardly here since Arabs themselves are also Semites.

2. It is well worth the reader's time to have a look at the Lebanese journalist's translated work, *The Crusades Through Arab Eyes,* which offers the other side of the story about this classic encounter that was so responsible for shaping early Muslim-Christian relations.

3. The colloquial Arabic term for automobile is "'arabiyya", or literally a thing that moves about.

6

Islamic Family Law: Social and Political Change

Islamic law is based on the holy sources of the Qur'ān and Sunna and is therefore a religious law in theory and in practice. The Qur'ān, as the revealed word of God, and Sunna, the teachings and the practice of the Messenger of God, Muḥammad, are fundamental sources that have been interpreted over the ages, but cannot be altered. Indeed various schools of interpretation have developed since the introduction of Islam, primarily in the first century after the Hijra (seventh to eighth centuries C.E.). These include the Māliki, Hanafī, Hanbalī, and Shafi'i, as well as others which are a bit more obscure, which have had their origins and influence in various parts of the original core of the early Islamic world. For example, the Māliki law grew out of the customs in practice in Medina and Mecca and spread throughout North and West Africa, while the Hanafī school spread with the Ottoman Empire. The differences in interpretation between the different schools are, relatively speaking, rather minor and do not represent doctrinal or factional differences in Islamic law.

Sharī'a, as a religious law, is comprehensive and theoretically applies to all legal matters that we would differentiate in the West as civil, criminal and family law. There is even a system of economics, banking, and finance that has grown out of Islamic prescriptions (discussed in chapters 5 and 7). In practice, in the modern period, Islamic Sharī'a has been circumscribed by Ottoman rule, which secularized much in commerce and trade, and which relegated the Sharī'a more to a law governing personal status matters of Muslims. The colonial powers reinforced and amplified this model, introduced their own Western laws in civil and criminal areas, and left Islamic law to govern family matters almost exclusively. Thus the current movement by the Islamists to restore the comprehensive role of the Sharī'a in Islamic society does have historical legitimacy. However, Western and some Muslim critics have raised a series of questions as to the compatibility of Islamic law with the standards and the demands of the modern state in terms of the protection of the rights of non-Muslims and women. This issue, too, is addressed in chapter 7.

Each of the countries of the Arab-Muslim Middle East share Islamic culture, and they share, to varying degrees, Arabic language and culture. Most are nations with a background of European colonialism: French rule in the case of the Maghrib and the Levant, Italian rule in Libya, and British rule in the cases of the Nile Valley countries of the Sudan and Egypt, Jordan, Palestine, Iraq and the oil nations of the Persian Gulf and Arabian Peninsula. Each country has been governed, since independence or the formation of a new nation, essentially by a monarchy or single party or military monopoly that has effectively excluded democratic elections or referenda on the subjects of family and social change, or on any other matter.

Although different in the particulars of the historical development of family law matters, the laws of each country all derive from a common Islamic base for the majorities of their respective populations, although each has religious and cultural minorities who have been historically exempted from Muslim family laws. Moreover, each country has been affected by developments in Muslim family law during the twentieth century, whereby the laws of marriage and divorce especially have been reformed and liberalized. During this period child betrothal has virtually disappeared, and the right of the woman, not her father, to choose her marriage partner has been supported in law. During this same time, the previous unilateral right of the husband to divorce has been seriously undermined, with a corresponding rise in the legal interpretation and actual practice of the wife's right to judicial divorce. This latter legal development rests with the Māliki religious interpretation that a wife should not be harmed in her marriage. The initial grounds that were recognized for women seeking divorce in court were injury or harm, at first interpreted as physical harm, such as beating, abandonment, or failure to support, but later incorporating notions of psychological abuse, such as insult. The right of a wife to be supported and the duty of a husband to support the family have been reinforced strongly in the recent decades of economic growth in some Arab-Muslim countries and relative stagnation in others. With massive labor migration from poorer to richer Arab countries, the stress placed on the family has been observed most acutely in the sharp rise in cases of nonsupport raised by wives against husbands who are labor migrants. One of the advantages of the world Muslim community (Umma) idea is that national boundaries can become irrelevant in Islamic family law cases, whereby Muslim courts of differing nations recognize subpoenas, decisions, and other official documents from other national Islamic courts.

Even though there are great commonalities in the religious law and practice of Muslim communities, nevertheless each nation has its own unique political developments, especially contemporarily in relation to the larger issue of secularism versus Islamic revival. The focus of this chapter is three separate and contrasting nations with regard to the development of family law and the degree to which this body of law has been affected by secular or Islamist trends over the past several decades. These countries are Tunisia, with a history of secular rule and a liberal (by Western standards) family law policy; Egypt, with a secular history of family law development but a growing Islamist movement; and the Sudan, with a secular history that was fundamentally altered when Islamic law (Sharī'a) was declared state law in 1983. Examination of these cases aids in the understanding of the complexities underlying Islamic society and family issues and reveals that there is no single, monolithic system of law governing all Islamic contexts.

Tunisia's first postindependence president, Habīb Bourgība, was among the pioneers, after Atatürk in Turkey, to revolutionize Islamic family law under an enlightened and liberal philosophy that promised to emancipate women through legal change. Today this secular approach to law and government is under question by Islamist forces who seek legal reform and restoration of the more traditional Sharī'a as part of a larger political agenda of Islamic revival. Egypt has a unified court system whereby Islamic family law is applied under the same general jurisdiction as its more Western-derived civil and criminal codes. However, Islamic revival has had a powerful impact upon Egyptian society, with a majority of young, educated women turning to an Islamic style of dress, and with increasing demand that Islamic law play a greater role in a reconstructed, more religiously based government. And in the Sudan, the military regime that seized power in 1989 has installed an Islamic government: since 1983, under the former military head of state Ja'afar al-Numayri, Islamic law has been state law. The family law was just codified in 1991, and only Islamic law is applied in all civil and criminal matters, a fact which has fanned the flames of the chronic civil war between the north and the south.

These countries represent points on a continuum of secular to Islam-ist approaches to law and government. The Sudan is an Islamic state with Sharī'a as national law, which alienates a significant portion of its population. Egypt is a secular state that retained intact most of the substance of Muslim family law, but it has a large Islamist movement pressing for a greater role for Islamic law in the state. Tunisia is a secular state that has significantly revised Islamic law in theory and in practice, but it has a growing Islamist trend that would return Sharī'a family law to its original status.

Islamic Law (Sharī'a)

Sharī'a in Arabic means the "path" or the "correct way," and in a reli-gious sense it is quite clear that this means adhering to a correctly guided life that is upright and conforming to the teachings and practice of Islam. It is the proper reference to the religious law of Islam. *Shar'i* is used in modern standard Arabic to refer to street names and correct roads to take when traveling to destinations. This is one of many exam-ples of the interpenetration of the sacred and secular in Islamic life, such as the frequently heard expressions in daily conversation dealing with the effect of God on one's everyday activities, like *"Insha' Allāh"* and *"al-Hamdulillah"*. Living in a *Shar'i* way can be used to describe a proper home for a husband and wife, or living with one's family and assisting them rather than living alone in a flat, or to describe the revived form of Islamic dress that many young Muslim women are adopting. All are examples of proper conduct guided by the religion of Islam. From an Islamic point of view, there is little distinction between sacred and secular, and the different contextual use of terms like *Shar'i* and *Sharī'a* is more noticeable to the Western non-Muslim than to the Muslim, for whom religion and society more comfortably commingle. The past de-velopment and future role of Islamic law in Muslim societies is a critical part of the contemporary debate regarding the "correct path" for Islamic nations to pursue into the twenty-first century.

Tunisia

Tunisia has most radically altered the traditional content of Islamic family law, and Tunisian law would experience the most dramatic change were the Islamist trend to become dominant.

The Islamization of the Maghrib figures prominently in Tunisian history with Kairouan being established as the center of Maghrib Islam after 670 C.E. The Zaytouna Mosque in Tunis became the center of higher Islamic studies, while throughout the country over 20,000 Islamic schools, or kuttabs, were established. Ottoman rule, overseen by the infamous corsairs, led the country into a crippling foreign debt that opened the way to French colonialism.

During French colonial rule, between 1888 and 1956, the historic Zaytouna Mosque and University was eclipsed by the secular, westernized Sidiqi College which produced a new breed of Francophone intellectuals. In 1932 a new law allowed Tunisians to acquire French nationality; this assimilation was backed by the highest religious authority, the Sheikh al-Islam and Mufti, who issued a fatwa permitting "French" Tunisians to remain Muslim as long as they performed their religious duties and were buried in Muslim cemeteries.

The nationalist leader Habīb Bourgība led the country to independence through the secular Dastour (Constitution) Party. The party's attitude toward Islam was revolutionary, and reforms were issued by decree without even pro forma approval of the Tunisian religious scholars, the 'Ulamā'. This contrasts markedly to developments in Egypt, where the powerful 'Ulamā', associated with the great international Al-Azhar University, has had an important role in both the colonial and postindependence states. This highlights the overall weakening of the Zaytouna Islamic University during colonialism and its lack of renewal after independence. In fact, Zaytouna Mosque and University was neutralized by government appointment of faculty and selection of imāms, with passive and ineffectual 'Ulamā' and was finally closed during Bougība's rule (Handal 1989). Instead of traditional interpretation by Tunisia's 'Ulamā', Bourgība used his personal interpretation of Islam, *ijtihād,* and tried to espouse its true spirit by moving away from orthodoxy of law.

Besides the changes in the family law described below, Bourgiba tried to do away with traditional Maghribi folk worship of saints, the marabout, and the wearing of the veil, both of which he viewed as symbols of the past. Family planning was seen as consistent with an Islamic view, and some of the most liberal programs favoring the limitation of family size were sponsored by the Tunisian government. More controversial was Bourqība's recommendation to end Ramaḍān fasting as part of a "jihad against underdevelopment" since fasting/feasting are expensive and inefficient. The Sharīʿa courts were integrated into a "modern" legal system, and Zaytouna University became a department at the newly created University of Tunis in 1961.

The new Code of Personal Status, ratified in 1956, became the most significant reform of newly independent Tunisia. Its most salient features included the abolition of polygamy, which was made punishable by prison and a fine of 24,000 dinars. This legal reform necessitated some explanation and a period of legal tolerance by the government. In 1964 the government issued an explanatory new decree regarding invalid marriages (polygamous marriages), whereby the court enforced the dower payment and established that the children of such marriages were the legitimate heirs to both their parents' lineages.

Divorce reforms were also controversial, with the recognition of the right of both wife and husband to initiate divorce. This radically altered the traditional unilateral right of the husband to divorce using the triple pronouncement without the intervention of the courts, and it required a court appearance for both parties in divorce cases. In 1968 this trend toward equalizing the legal roles of men and women was carried further. The right for the wife to seek employment or choose a profession demanding work outside of the home was established without the necessity of prior permission of her husband.

Amended again in 1981, the law granted the divorced woman priority in the custody of the children and all legal maintenance (nafaqa) to which she was accustomed in married life, which continues as a debt upon the husband's resources even until his death, with payment to stop only if the condition of the woman improves. This unleashed something of a backlash against the reform movement as having gone too far, and the topic still provoked animated discussion when I raised the subject in 1990. Critics at the time contended that it unfairly discriminated against men and placed them on the defensive. A part of the backlash resulting from the reformed divorce law came from women judges, lawyers, and educators as well as from male legal professionals. Divorce cases initiated by women increased while cases raised by men also increased (Sherif-Stanford 1984: 93), so it might be inferred that the divorce reform had an initial destabilizing effect resulting in more divorce, rather than what was perhaps the intention of the law—to inhibit divorce by men.

Also arranged marriage was abolished, and a legal age of twenty-one for the groom and eighteen years for the bride was established in law. Mahr was greatly reduced in legal status and explicitly made the legal property of the wife, while the wife's right to refuse cohabitation if the mahr is not paid according to negotiated amounts and time of payments was reaffirmed.

Added to these revolutionary changes, Bourgība and his reformers attacked the veil as a symbol of female subordination. Moreover, the French language was made the official language of instruction, and Bourgība promoted a Franco-Tunisian synthesis and a Mediterranean Islam. Emphasis was placed on modern education, and literacy rates dramatically increased, while the percentage of girls attending school rose to 40 percent.

Regarding property and inheritance, support was given to the Islamic principle that the husband has no right to control his wife's property, estates, or earnings. However, the wife may contribute to the family budget if she desires. This was amended in 1968 to state that the "wife is her husband's responsibility no matter what her economic condition," and if the husband is away, she can legally demand that support from her husband. This has marked bearing upon the large number of men who migrate abroad for work, especially to France and other European countries, and whose families may suffer economic hardship as a result.

The inheritance code follows traditional Islamic law regarding female inheritance, which is half that of male heirs, but does make the children, the wife, and the grandparents the primary heirs. Only if these heirs are not available does the estate revert to more traditional Muslim inheritance, where other members of the extended family are included. This had the effect of strengthening nuclear family ties and lineal ties between parents and children, over the broader Islamic concept of the extended family.

Optional legal wills are possible, written and registered with the Ministry of Justice for leaving property to people, charities, and religious shrines provided that such assets do not exceed the Islamic bequeathable third. In one study (Sherif-Stanford 1984: 90), two-thirds of Tunisians interviewed said they have left the optional one-third to wives, daughters, mothers, and sisters who would otherwise inherit one-half or less than their male relatives, suggesting a societal response to changes in family life.

The Tunisian Code of Personal Status was issued at the time of national independence when the desire for change and modernization was at its height. However, it was not achieved by political mobilization and activism of women, although many women were significant leaders in the struggle for Tunisian independence (Labidi 1990). Instead these radical changes in the law were introduced by fiat, by decree from above at the presidential level. Bourgība himself created the National Union of Tunisian Women (UNFT) to "pursue the task of liberating women from ignorance and illiteracy," and he referred to the members as *mujahidat* or fighters in a holy war against these (Sherif-Stanford 1984: 83).

For all of its modernization and liberalization affecting the status of women, the UNFT received the United Nations award for outstanding achievement in human rights, and Kurt Waldheim cited Tunisia as an example to other Arab societies. Bourgība and legal reform are inextricably linked, as shown by the fact that the commemoration of the institution of the Personal Status Code and Bourgība's birthday are traditionally celebrated on the same day.

Although Tunisia is often hailed at the single most progressive Arab-Muslim state in the area of women's rights and legal reform, this liberal tradition has not been reflected in the participation of women in politics. Despite a women's union with an estimated 100,000 members, Tunisian women have been minimally involved in public life, except for a few prominent members of the Bourgība family (Waltz, 1988: 2). This lack of grass-roots participation by women in their own emancipation underscores the weakness of revolution or reform from the top down.

More recently, Islamic revival has become a feature of contemporary Tunisian politics, with its inevitable ramifications in social policy recommendations. Unlike the Bourgībist reform movement, it has mobilized young women in significant numbers. The first organized Islamist activity was *Ittijah al-Islami,* which evolved to become the al-Nahḍa, or Renaissance, Party. Its main thesis is that economic and social development must take into account religious values.

Al-Nahḍa relies on Qur'ān and Sunna as fundamental sources but rejects "doctrinal sectarianism" and tolerates differences of opinion. Followers reject the idea of class conflict, seeing the overriding power of the Umma as a great unifier. However, the movement allies itself with the poor and has its greatest mass following there.

With respect to law, not surprisingly, al-Nahḍa sees a great disparity between Islamic Sharī'a and the law as applied in Tunisia today. To bring about change, the Islamist task is to resocialize the masses and

Al-Nahḍa political rally in Tunisia, where Islamists call for the restoration of Sharī'a in Tunisian government and law.

then establish the Islamic order, based on democracy and *shuṙa,* or consultation (Shahin 1990). Al-Nahḍa calls upon the Tunisian people to fight the Jāhiliya (period of ignorance before Islam) which has been created by Bourgība and his successor, Ben-Ali. They see the Tunisian Code of Personal Status as a revision and not a reform of Islamic Sharī'a. Another Islamist group, al-Da'wa, rejects the code as un-Islamic, coming from man not God, and refers to it as the "pagan government's code" (Magnuson 1987: 204).

Al-Nahḍa has called for the return of polygyny, which is basic in religious law and allowable as an extraordinary, not ordinary, measure. Some have called for the return of women from working outside of the home to domestic life; others have denounced *ikhtilāt,* open socializing between men and women. Female members of al-Nahḍa, using the model of the Iranian revolution where women fought with men against imperialism, have demanded revision of the idea about women working and say that women are needed as doctors, nurses, and teachers to work with girls.

Al-Nahḍa is a movement led by educated, disaffected young Tunisians, with high participation of women, thus challenging the secular idea that Islam is against women's rights. Reviving the practice of the Sharī'a is the goal of the movement, but this is to be achieved primarily through education. Al-Nahḍa members are critical of the older Egyptian Muslim Brotherhood movement because they are less democratic than the Palestinian movement, for example, which has given greater opportunities for women to participate and lead.

The overall picture on personal status law and the current political situation is that most Tunisian 'Ulamā', in addition to the Islamists, call for review of the Code of Personal Status, with polygyny a central issue. Most Islamists agree that maintaining polygyny is an unalterable part of Sharī'a that should be restored. The progressive Islamists argue that the main point is to safeguard the family, rather than to protect polygyny as an absolute right. As for Islamic dress or other outward signs of personal religious conviction, these should be a matter of choice for women.

Tunisia is an example of legal reform in the family law area from the top down, one of the most radical and revolutionary changes in the Sharī'a family law since the massive changes imposed by Atatürk in Turkey in 1926. To the degree that one-party, one-man rule has become unpopular in Tunisia and the Islamic path represents an apparently democratic alternative, the issue of increasing Islamization and the restoration of Sharī'a remains alive.

Egypt

After independence in 1952, Egypt retained traditional Sharī'a in the law of personal status, while it combined the Sharī'a family law with French- and English-derived codes of civil and criminal law into a single system. The personal status courts have separate facilities but are administered as part of a comprehensive system of Egyptian law.

Historically, the Sharī'a was the law in effect from the early times of the introduction of Islam into Egypt during its first great century of expansion. From the Ottoman period, after the fifteenth century of the common era, Sharī'a remained in effect until the nineteenth century, when legal reform introduced Western-inspired codes in all areas except the law of personal status. During English colonialism Egyptian family law was left unchanged until the family law reforms of 1920 and 1929. At the same time the Egyptian feminist movement focused, among other issues, on the reform of Muslim marriage and divorce laws (Phillip 1978: 290).

Law 25 (1920) and Law 25 (1929) drew upon various schools of Islamic jurisprudence, *madhāhib,* and introduced judicial divorce initiated by women because of desertion or lack of maintenance by her husband or his incarceration or terminal illness. In addition, restrictions were placed on a husband's right of repudiation of the marriage by pronouncement of *ṭalāq* (divorce), making sure that it must be a clear, sober, and deliberate decision. The reforms of 1920 and 1929 left out draft proposals on the restriction of polygyny, with King Fuad refusing to support the controversial recommendation to limit plural marriages and families that husbands could not maintain adequately (Esposito 1982: 60).

The new constitution in 1956 gave women and men equal public rights, established suffrage for women, and gave them the right to hold state offices at all levels.

Recommendations to amend the family law were proposed by the Ministry of Social Affairs in 1943, 1945, and 1969, and each time they failed (Esposito 1982: 60). Proposals to reform the male right to polygyny and certain aspects of the divorce laws were advanced in 1960, when the governments of Egypt and Syria formed the United Arab Republic and merged elements of Syrian and Egyptian laws. The abolition of *bayt al-ṭaʿa,* the right of a husband to retrieve by police force a wife who has fled the conjugal home, was proposed, but it was adamantly opposed by the Egyptian 'Ulamā', and in any event the issue was made moot by the end of union of the two countries.

In 1966 the proposal to abolish *bayt al-ṭaʿa* was again proposed by reformers, along with eleven other amendments to 1929 law. These additional reforms included the obligation of the husband to pay the wife's medical expenses; the wife's right to stipulate in the marriage contract that she can be employed; the husband's restriction on taking a second wife without the permission of the first wife; attempted reconciliation by family councils prior to litigation in divorce cases; temporary maintenance for a wife before legal proceedings; divorce only after reconciliation attempts fail; a year of additional support for a divorced woman; invalidation of repudiation by an irate husband; polygyny constituting an injury to the first wife and potential grounds for divorce; remarriage not nullifying a woman's right to custody of her children; and child visitation after divorce as an act of love and not to take place in a police station, as had been the practice. The political pressure of the Arab-Israeli war of 1967 forced the government to shelve the controversial proposal, but this only deferred the issues (Najjar 1986: 5). Gamal Abdel Nasser was quoted as saying in regard to the difficulty of reforming the family law, "I would like to do what Bourgība has done but the obstacles are greater here in the heart of Islam at the gate of Al-Azhar" (Handal, 1989).

Bayt al-ṭaʿa was finally abolished in 1967 by a ministerial decree of the Minister of Justice, with specific mention being made of a ban on the issuance of an order of obedience by force. The decree was immediately challenged by the National Assembly as an inappropriate method of changing the law, and there was controversy and resistance among the judges, many of whom refused to comply with the new order (Fluehr-Lobban and Bardsley-Sirois 1990: 41). There was lively debate in the Assembly, but few members were willing to go on record as supporting the rule of obedience by police action and the matter ended there.

In 1970 after the death of Nasser, the assumption of power by Anwar al-Sādāt pushed the issues of personal status law reform into the background. The growing strength of the Muslim conservatives was felt keenly by Sādāt. After the subject of the future status of the Sharīʿa was openly debated in 1975 within the Arab Socialist Union, the conservatives were successful in advancing the view that the Sharīʿa alone would constitute the basis of any reform of Egyptian law.

The most innovative legal reform of the family law since independence was put forward by Sādāt in 1979 in Law 44, widely referred to as "Jehan's law" because of the influence of Mrs. Jehan Sādāt on the development of the various proposals. In fact, the changes had been discussed at least since 1971 when the Minister of Social Affairs, Dr. Aisha Ratib, chaired the Committee for the Revision of Family Law which made many of the recommendations embodied in the 1979 law. Law 44 was struck down as unconstitutional in 1985, having been made law in an illegal, nonparliamentary fashion by Sādāt. Revoking the law meant a return to the 1929 Code of Personal Status, out of step with modern times but hailed as a victory by the Islamists.

Even conservatives realized that returning to the 1929 law was counterproductive, and following the assassination of Sādāt in 1981 by Muslim extremists, the way was prepared for some compromise. The new president, Hosni Mubarak, pushed through the People's Assembly another set of amendments, Law 100 of 3 July 1985, which was basically a revised version of the 1979 law, but yielded to some of the demands of the conservatives.

Some of the major provisions of Law 44 are as follows: 1) It insured proper registration of divorce with a notary public (*muwāthiq*) or by husband's acknowledgment (*iqrār*), stressing knowledge and information for both parties, so the husband could not divorce without the wife's knowledge; 2) A second marriage constituted an injury (*ḍarar*) to the first wife and was grounds for divorce, even if not stipulated in the marriage contract; 3) The mother was favored as custodial parent by giving her the right to the conjugal dwelling during the period of custody; 4) The wife was entitled to legal separation if continued married life caused her unbearable harm; 5) Conditions under which the wife was entitled to maintenance were liberalized, and she had the right to divorce if maintenance ceased; 6) The wife was entitled to an indemnity (*mutʿa*) over and above the legal support (*nafaqa*) to which she was entitled in the event she had been repudiated without her consent or without apparent cause on her part (cited in Najjar 1986).

The law was hailed by feminists and liberals as a significant landmark toward the liberation of women. However, anticipating opposition from Muslim conservatives in 1979, Sādāt secured the endorsement of the law by a number of 'Ulamā' from the Academy of Islamic Research, the Al-Azhar Fatwa Committee, and judges of the Sharīʿa courts. All concurred that the law was in conformity with Sharīʿa principles and Islamic jurisprudence, in addition to being conducive to social justice and family harmony.

The Muslim Brotherhood strenuously objected, disputing the authenticity of the state-controlled 'Ulamās' endorsement. Their attack on the entire law focused on the denial of the husband's right to polygyny. They claimed that to do so would be to repudiate Islam, and the interpretation that this would be a harm to the first wife insinuates that the Prophet and his companions, the Saheban, permitted injury.

The government responded that all provisions had emanated from the fundamental sources of the Sharīʿa. Further, they had been drawn from a law of personal status that had been jointly approved by the combined People's Assemblies of Egypt and the Sudan (during the years when the two governments pursued a policy of political integration). Finally, they argued that the law was drawn up by recognized scholars

127

and had been approved by the Sheikh of al-Azhar, the Minister of Awqaf and the Mufti of Egypt.

A major constitutional challenge to the legislation regarding polygyny was filed in 1983. Various religious sheikhs, including Sheikh Saleh Abu Ismail, and Sheikh Gad al-Haqq, the Mufti of Egypt at the time and later Rector of Al-Azhar, argued that according to Māliki law injury can be caused by desertion, beating, and insulting, but not by marriage to another woman. The wife seeking divorce can always resort to *khul'* (mutual, negotiated divorce), which is preferable to *tafrīq* (separation by court order).

The innovative *muta'a*—an amount of money due to the divorced wife and justified as a divorce transition benefit that extends beyond the few months of support due to the wife during the normal three-month *'idda* period—was seen as a benevolence that would find favor in the eyes of God. Qur'ānic texts and jurists have supported muta'a compensation, but left the matter "to the wealthy according to his means and the poor according to his means" (Sura 2: 236). But the law now recognizes that times have changed and that a woman's welfare can no longer be left to a man's sense of honor and obligation. The courts determine the amount of the *muta'a* depending on the husband's condition and the circumstances of the divorce.

During parliamentary debate on the legislation, Sheikh Saleh voiced his opposition, "What has the husband done to deserve all this retribution? By divorcing his wife he acts according to God's ordinances!" And then invoking what was to him the worst example of a travesty on the Sharī'a law, he asks, "Do we want to become like Tunis which has abolished polygamy but condones concubinage?" (Najjar 1986: 22).

The proposals for changes in the custody law were almost equally controversial, and they were subjected to popular scrutiny and criticism beyond that emanating from the Islamists. Law 44 provided that the divorced wife with custody of minor children would be given exclusive right to the rented conjugal dwelling for the duration of the custody, unless the husband/father provided them with another appropriate residence. Custody was extended to fifteen years for a boy and the age of marriage for a girl, if the best interests of the children were served by being with their mother. The mother would not continue to receive support under these conditions. This was based on the Hanafi interpretation that it is the responsibility of the father to provide the custodial mother with a residence. The possibility of the custodial mother/ex-wife receiving *muta'a* for two years, using the conjugal home, and having custody of the children was seen by much of the public as legal reform having gone too far. It produced some of the most abrasive exchanges within the People's Assembly because of Egypt's "suffocating housing crisis." The law was portrayed "as a sword drawn over the husbands' necks" forcing them to obey their wives (*Al-Akbar*, 11 May 1985).

Charges were made that the law had been imposed by pressure from Anwar al-Sādāt, with Mrs. Sādāt alleged to be in the background. Some of its former supporters admitted after the assassination of Sādāt to having been pressured. Other judges in the family courts complained that Law 44 increased divorce litigation and it generated new disputes over muta'a and the matter of postdivorce residence in the former conjugal home. Ultimately Law 44 was annulled as unconstitutional on 4 May 1985, thus reinforcing the political principle that the People's Assembly, not the president, is the primary legislative power in Egypt.

After the annulment, various political groups that had promoted the legal reforms organized the Committee for the Defense of Women and the Family to oppose the return to the 1929 law and to mobilize support for immediate enactment of new legislation that would reinstate the substance and essential features of Law 44. Feminists, such as the journalist and publisher, Amina al Said, argued that Islam, properly understood, confers equal rights for women. Growing and open Islamist sentiment in the 1980s among many urban, educated Egyptian women dulled the anticipated enthusiastic response of women to this feminist agitation.

It was clear, even to those who opposed the 1979 law, that return to the 1929 law was untenable. Hosni Mubarak was clearly torn between a "modern," secular approach to legal reform and the growing power of the Islamic resurgence. A compromise came about in 1985 with Revised Law 100, which reinstated most of the substance of Law 44, except for two concessions. Responding to the constitutional challenge mounted earlier, Law 100 declared that the second marriage does not necessarily constitute harm to the first wife. Under Law 100 the burden of proof is on the wife to demonstrate the harm, physical or psychological. If not proven, she can be divorced, but is not entitled to muta'a, a benefit or compensation that can only be awarded by a judge in cases of proven harm or abuse (*ṭalāq al-ḍarar*).

As part of the compromise legislation, the husband is still obliged to provide adequate rental housing to his divorced wife who is the custodian of their minor children, but he has the exclusive right to his dwelling, which he owns as his private property and which he provided at the time of the marriage. Further, upon her loss of the right to custody the wife loses the right to the residence, so the primacy of the welfare of the children is favored over the financial condition of the divorced wife. Without children, the divorced wife must depend on her parents or relatives, and failing them, there is no government safety net or welfare program. With the government officially promoting family planning and the reduction of family size, the message of the revised law to married women is that larger families and minor children may provide legal and financial security.

Egypt is clearly a nation and a society torn between its secular political history since independence under Nasser, Sādāt and Mubarak, and its intensifying Islamist movement, which has both popular roots and a powerful legitimizing authority coming from the center of Muslim learning at Al-Azhar University. The Egyptian legislature and courts have attempted to steer a middle course between the conservative Islamists and the reformist, modernizing secularists.

Sudan

The Sudanese converted to Islam later than either Egypt or Tunisia, with Muslim kingdoms and a significant spread of the religion taking place only after the fifteenth century of the common era. The Funj Kingdom at Sinnar was the first to install Islamic courts and have religious teachers and interpreters of the Sharī'a. Cultural and religious influence of Islam penetrated Bilād as-Sudan more from the west than from either the Nile Valley or Red Sea routes. Christian kingdoms in Nubia halted the spread of Islam south from Egypt until their fall in fifteenth century. However, the African pilgrimage route to the holy places passed through the Sudan. The pilgrims from West Africa provided a continuous infusion of Islamic religion and customs since the first Islamic states.

The West African influence of Islamic tradition brought with it Māliki customs and law, an interpretation grounded in everyday practice in Mecca after the introduction of Islam. Ottoman conquest and administration of the Sudan after 1821 brought Hanafī law, where it blended with local interpretation and practice not only in Sudan, but also in Egypt and other parts of the Ottoman Empire in Africa. The success of the Mahdist uprising in the later part of the nineteenth century, an uprising as much against the abusive administration and corrupt practice of Islam by the Ottoman Turks as it was against European intrusion, brought the first independent Islamic republic, which lasted from 1885 to 1898. Following British reconquest, colonial rule lasted from 1898 to 1956, during which time "Mohammedan law" was relegated to the arena of personal status law alone, but administered throughout the Muslim regions of the country through a separate system of courts. I have written extensively about the development of Sharī'a law in the twentieth century in the Sudan (see Fluehr-Lobban 1983, 1987), and I offer the following summary of the major points which characterized its application until the Islamization of the law in 1983. Making Sharī'a law state law has precipitated renewed civil war and deepened the political crisis in the Sudan up to the present time.

The Sudan was one of the first dominantly Muslim nations in the twentieth century to modify the traditional unilateral right of the husband to divorce, and to introduce the right to a judicial divorce by a woman. A clear continuation of this legal trend is evident in the Tunisian abolition of this right of the husband to divorce by repudiation in the early 1960s. The Sudanese Judicial Circular 17 (ca. 1915) opened "the door of interpretation" in family matters regarding the potential for harm or abuse of the wife in a marriage, consistent with Mālikī interpretation that such harm is contrary to Islam and social harmony. Divorce initiated by women is permitted on the grounds of physical cruelty (ṭalāq al-ḍarar) and desertion by the husband (ṭalāq khawf al-fitna). Beyond this, the law, as presented in Circular 17, provides a procedure and means for the wife to obtain maintenance payments (nafaqa) from the husband who is absent for any reason, or from the husband who has failed to maintain his wife adequately. This lack of support is viewed as a source of harm to the wife.

Many of these reforms anticipated developments that were not to occur in Egypt until the Family Law Reform of 1929; indeed most of the Grand Qadis of the Sudan, appointed by the English during colonial times, were Egyptian, and they may have tested these reforms first in the Sudan before their introduction in Egypt. The major mechanism for modification and interpretation of the law has been the judicial circulars which have been issued by the Grand Qadis until the courts were merged in 1980 and the position of Grand Qadi was eliminated. The judicial circulars had the effect of law.

The broad principle of protecting the wife against harm in the marriage is a rich one, and was built upon again in 1973, after independence, in Circular 59, which recognized mental cruelty as another form of harm and thus grounds for divorce (Fluehr-Lobban 1983: 88).

The right of a Muslim husband to divorce his wife by triple pronouncement, ideally on three separate occasions separated by three-month intervals, was long recognized as subject to abuse, especially by ṭalāq ṭalāta, the triple pronouncement of divorce made on a single occasion, often in a fit of rage or under the influence of alcohol. The Sudan followed Egypt in 1935 by making the triple pronouncement illegal and by making a formal legal requirement of three separate and deliberate declarations of divorce.

The wife's right to marital support, particularly if the husband is absent, was safeguarded in law, and the issue of consent in marriage was addressed. In 1935 the strict Hanafī rule that an underage or adult woman could be betrothed with only the consent of the male marriage guardian, usually the father, was reaffirmed. By 1960, under feminist pressure, this was reformed to make full and express consent to marriage the right of the woman

As in Egypt, a similar retraction of bayt al-ṭā'a was instituted in the Sudan in 1970 by Ja'afar al-Numayri as part of a package of presidential decrees improving the status of women. There was a favorable response by women's organizations and only slight resistance from the judiciary.

An early reform in the law regarding custody of children, in 1931, went beyond Egypt's Family Law of 1929. Using Mālikī instead of Hanafī interpretations, a divorced mother was allowed to retain custody of her son, beyond the usual seven years, to the time of puberty, while the custody of the daughter may be extended from nine years to the time of the consummation of her marriage.

Sharī'a law in the Sudan had a separate and unique means of development through the use of judicial circulars throughout most of the twentieth century, and represented an enlightened approach to family law issues. During the sixteen years of al-Numayri's military rule (1969–1985), dramatic developments affected the future of Sharī'a law in the country. The civil and Sharī'a courts were combined in 1980, and shortly

Gathering of Egyptian and Sudanese 'Ulamā' in Khartoum in advance of the Islamization of law in 1983.

after, in 1983, al-Numayri made Islamic law state law, despite the negative impact this was certain to have on the large non-Muslim population of the south. Civil war broke out again in the south in 1983 over this issue and has continued to this day, with a central point being the withdrawal of the state-imposed Islamic law. Al-Numayri was overthrown in 1985 and succeeding governments have failed to resolve the issue. Since 1989 an Islamist government has been in power and has reasserted the supremacy of Sharī'a in the country, while secessionist sentiments in the southern movement have been revived and the future of the nation appears in jeopardy.

The current Islamist military government, with a civil war raging and an unpopular international record on human rights, nonetheless turned its attention to the area of family law only six months after seizing power in June 1989. In January 1990 the Conference on the Role of Women in National Salvation recommended that a code of personal status law be drafted. A legislative committee drew up the 1991 Act on Personal Law for Muslims, which was passed by the ruling military and the Council of Ministers and came into effect on 24 July 1991. The new code brings together in five volumes the collective wisdom of Islamic family law in the Sudan dealing with marriage, divorce, guardianship and property, trusts, gifts and entertainment, inheritance, loans, and relations with relatives.

This first codification of the personal status law is not innovative, but it does put into a single set of books the background and interpretations of legal development in the Sudan. It consistently favors Māliki interpretations over Hanafī law, and it makes explicit points in the law that had previously only been decided in high court cases.

For example, it recognizes the woman's increased authority in marriage and expressly rejects the six conditions to be met in Hanafī law for a valid marriage to be effected; religion, freedom, job or craft, financial situation, place of residence, and reasonable pedigree. These conditions when applied in Sudan created many ethnic and racial problems, especially over the issues of pedigree and parentage, with several famous cases of objections by marriage guardians to future sons-in-law with alleged slavery in their backgrounds (see Fluehr-Lobban 1987: 127–129). The new law requires only mutual respect between the two families; the financial situation of the families is also removed, such that competence in marriage can only be measured by "the practice of religion and good morals" (El-Rasoul 1991: 29).

The new law widens the concept of nafaqa in marriage to include education and medical treatment of the wife, which were excluded under the previous Hanafī interpretation. A new ruling was instituted regarding engagement gifts; previously if the engagement was broken, the gifts had to be returned, according to the Hanafī school. Under the new code, if the fiancé breaks off the engagement without reasonable cause, the gifts do not have to be returned, consistent with Māliki law.

Matters regarding domestic possessions and furniture are also treated flexibly in the new code, taking into consideration the development of Sudanese society. Previously, if the husband and wife disputed over the marital possessions, what was considered appropriate for the man would go to the man, and likewise suitable property was awarded to the woman. Thus women were typically granted only their clothes and jewelry. Because it is not clear any longer what is suitable possession to man or woman, the new code provides for the division of possessions equally between them (El-Rasoul 1991: 29).

The major drafter of the code, Sheikh Siddiq Abdel Hai, believes that the code will have a positive effect on the unification of the sources of the law and will bring about an end to the conflict and contradictions that occurred in the past in balancing the Hanafī and Mālikī schools. Clearly set out in easily comprehensible language, the new personal status code can save the time of judges and lawyers, who now have a ready reference to many questions.

Tunisia, Egypt, and the Sudan Compared

In each country we have examined, the issue of Islamic law is a central political one, whether it is to be limited to family matters alone, or whether it commands or will command a greater role in state law and government. Sharī'a law and its future place in each of these predominantly Muslim nations has become a major part of the dialogue and, increasingly, of the political confrontation, between Islamists of various types and their secularist opponents. Under Islamist pressure, Egypt has formally taken the position that the Sharī'a constitutes *the* source of legislation for the country. The Sudan had taken a similar step even before Islamic law was made state law, bowing to growing Islamist pressures. Tunisia, with its dramatically secularized Islamic family law, is faced with a potentially powerful Islamist movement that seeks to restore the Sharī'a to its rightful place in a Muslim society.

While issues of family law may seem less important than the place of Sharī'a in state politics, in fact many of the battles between Islamist and secular reformers have been waged within the boundaries of Islamic family law. The British colonial authorities favored a policy that gave autonomy to the development of Islamic law in Egypt and the Sudan, in contrast to the direct method of colonial rule adopted by the French. With the 'Ulamā' retained in positions of religious and legal power, the development of Islamic family law in Egypt and the Sudan was slow and deliberate, proceeding along a basically Islamic path. However, the 'Ulamā' in Tunisia were already weakened and neutralized by the colonial state before Bourgība introduced his sweeping reforms, so he had little to fear from their opposition and little tradition of reform to build upon. It has been left to a new generation of activists, inspired by Islamic revival but not lead by any of the traditional 'Ulamā' to challenge the Bourgība legacy.

In all three countries certain areas of the law were more accommodating to legal reform and change than others. The relative ease and ready acceptance of the elimination of the triple pronouncement of divorce in each country suggests a broad consensus on the need to limit the potential and real abuse that had resulted from unilateral and hasty divorce of wives in this fashion. Likewise the recognition of the woman's right to initiate divorce and to be divorced on the commonly recognized grounds of economic neglect, desertion, and harm demonstrates wide agreement. The strengthening of the wife's right to maintenance and its enforcement has not been challenged, nor has the extension of the period of the mother's custody of her children after divorce.

However, the caution with which the subject of polygyny has been approached in Egypt and the controversy over its limited restriction reveal the sensitive nature of this issue. The abolition of polygyny in Tunisia was, perhaps, the most notable and internationally recognized feature of the package of reforms undertaken there. The abolition of polygyny has not been a serious part of the agenda for legal reform in the Sudan, and has historically appeared only in feminist tracts. However, rates of polygyny are extremely low in all three countries and have been declining throughout the Arab and Islamic worlds throughout the consecutive decades of the twentieth century. The confrontations over the abolition, restriction, or retention of polygyny have been more symbolic than real. Fruitful arguments have ensued over the question of whether a practice specifically mentioned in the Qur'ān as permissible can be seen as wrong, or can be amended. This formed the basis of the constitutional challenge by Islamist forces to the restriction on polygyny in Egypt under Law 44, which said that the husband must seek the permission of the first wife before taking a second. And this is the basis for the Islamist disapproval of the Tunisian ban on polygyny.

Such legal reform also has a political dimension. During the nationalist and early postindependence periods in Egypt and the Sudan, feminist agitation for reform of the family law played an important role in setting the agenda for sociolegal change. Although women were active in nationalist mobilization in Tunisia, emancipation and women's rights came by decree, with an agenda that was synthesized by President Bourgība who saw himself as the liberator of his country's backward traditions. Anwar al-Sādāt's less dramatic effort at reform, in Law 44, was ultimately undermined by his failure to work through legislative channels.

The politics of Islamic revival are closely related to this broader discussion of family law. Islamist pressure forced al-Sādāt's successor, Hosni Mubarak, to reformulate Law 44, with major concessions made to Islamist objections. Leaders of the Muslim Brotherhood (after 1985, the National Islamic Front) in the Sudan persuaded al-Numayri to declare Islamic law as state law in 1983, despite the drastic political consequences for the country. The same forces have blocked any challenge to remove or modify this decision by presidential fiat in the years since Numayri's overthrow. Now in power, the National Islamic Front vows never to retreat on the issue of Sharīʿa, and no constitutional challenge as to the legality of the process by which Islamic law became state law is likely under the current Islamist regime.

Matters of family law affect all citizens of a nation, and when the fundamentals of the law derive from a religious base, as in Muslim societies, the sensibilities aroused can be of a deeply personal and spiritual nature. The dynamics of family law reform in the three countries examined reflect a complex blend of social, religious, and political change in the twentieth century. The role of Islam and its basic institutions, the status of women and the family, and the relationship of the family to the modern Muslim state are among the most pressing issues of the day.

Changing Family Patterns

From a social scientific perspective, the changes in family law are reflective of changes that have been taking place in Islamic society for some time. These are especially dramatic with respect to the status of women, for whom major social change has been under way in the twentieth century, especially in the decades since the advent of independence.

Most impressive has been the entry of women into the work force. Women represent significant numbers where the economic need is the greatest, but educated middle-class women have entered into the professions in ever-increasing numbers as well. Egypt and Tunisia have the greatest number of women in the work force—that is, women undertaking salaried employment outside of the home—at about 25 percent. Even in a country as traditionally conservative as the Sudan, the participation of women in the work force has doubled in the past decade, from 7 percent to 15 percent of all women. This may seem low by Western standards, where typically well over 50 percent of women work outside of the home for wages. But similar economic and social forces are at work in the Arab-Muslim world, and are occurring perhaps at a more rapid pace than what was witnessed in the West. Because according to traditional values such work by women is considered shameful, it was usually undertaken only under the direst of economic and social conditions. Historically, women driven to work by personal circumstances were looked upon as the most pitiable of humans. The idea that women might work in factories, in government or business offices, or in gender-mixed situations was unthinkable only a generation or two ago. But the shame is beginning to be replaced with a sense of dignity in work, and many women have entered professions thought of as "male", such as engineering, medicine, or law.

Of course, all women work, as do all men, whether they reside in the urban centers or in the countryside. Apart from the domestic work, growing numbers of women are working in the informal economic sector as street vendors, maids and domestics, or in craft production (often for items which sell on the domestic or international market, such as carpetweaving). This work, although described as self-employment, places women in highly dependent positions whereby their livelihood or supplement to family income depends upon their relations with economic middlemen or those who hire them unofficially. Needless to say the transience, vulnerability, and lack of benefits that a person working in the informal sector receives represent hardships for these working women. Despite oftentimes difficult working conditions, the entry of women into the informal sector is an offshoot of the larger social transformation that has brought women into the formal working sector.

This economic participation of women amounts to a social transformation in the postindependence period, and to be sure, it correlates highly with the era of secular politics and the state support for the emancipation of women. In the current Islamist period, the propriety of women in the work force is under intense scrutiny. This trend is discussed more fully in chapter 7.

An interesting survey of 500 Sudanese women with an average age of twenty-six years and ten years of marriage was conducted under the auspices of the Ahfad University College for Women (Grotberg and Washi 1991), a pioneer in women's education in the Sudan and in the Muslim world generally. Although the majority (60 percent of these women married traditionally, that is, they married their first cousins, usually their father's brother's son), 13 percent were salaried employees. Those who indicated that they exercised personal choice in the selection of their husbands had significantly lower fertility rates. These women had, on average, 3.5 children, while the general fertility rate for Muslim Sudanese women is 6.0 children. In contrast, the ideal "modern" family is described by these women as having two children. The average educational level of women in the sample was intermediate or middle school, and their husbands were generally better educated, with an average of some secondary school training.

Family Planning Movement

An untutored Western response to fundamentalism in the Muslim world is a projection onto that social reality of the forces at work in one's own society. Thus fundamentalism in the Islamic world might suggest a ban or hostility toward birth control and family planning, as that issue has divided liberal and conservative religion in the West. In fact, there has been no comparable right to life movement in the Muslim world, and family planning and birth control information have entered Islamic society without much rancorous theological or political struggle. The accepted religious interpretation of the beginning of life is at the time of "quickening," or the time when the mother feels life in her body. Thus abortion in the early stages of the development of the fetus is not a moral problem, *per se.* However, if that abortion is linked to immoral and illicit sexual conduct, then the consequences are grave. Indeed, because sexual activity is so controlled and constrained in the Muslim world, the emphasis in birth control has been placed on prevention of pregnancy within the context of a married woman's life. The idea that birth control information and devices should be made available to unmarried women is anathema to every basic value of Islamic society and sexuality.

The family planning movement has entered Arab-Muslim society, generally speaking, as a by-product of the movement for female emancipation, which in turn was linked to the nationalist movements. Family planning clinics initially were introduced with the idea that the full incorporation of women's labor and participation in the newly independent nation required smaller families.

In the case of the three nations we have been examining, family planning movements were enthusiastically endorsed and promoted by the official women's organizations, the National Union of Tunisian Women, the Sudanese Women's Union, and the Egyptian Women's Union. To assist the working woman, accessible and inexpensive day care centers were also established by these womens' organizations. For urban, relatively better-educated working women, family size did decrease. However, in Egypt, where family planning was embraced as government policy and the emphasis shifted to rural women reducing the number of pregnancies, the results were far less successful. Egypt became recognized as an exception to the usual rule that urbanization curtails family size; large numbers of Egyptian peasants were streaming into Egypt's cities and still fellahin women were bearing an average of seven children. Government propaganda and international financial aid for family planning programs instilled questions about motives in the minds of many Egyptians, and the government got the message that the limited success and unenthusiastic response from people was a form of passive resistance. The programs then shifted to a more decentralized approach, involving local women cooperating with family planning clinics, without the apparent heavy hand of the government, and a greater success rate has been achieved.

Numerous studies have shown that the most effective way to reduce population is to promote education for women. There is a powerful and persuasive correlation between the number of years of a woman's education and the number of her children. The correlation is an inverse one: the greater the educational level, the fewer the children. In Grotberg and Washi's study of young married Sudanese women, lower fertility rates correlate not only with education, but also with the following set of attitudes: 1) a belief that a man and a woman can be friends; 2) that strict segregation of the sexes can be relaxed; 3) that a woman can choose to work outside of the home; 4) women can be involved in politics; and 5) women and men are equally competent and should enjoy full equal rights in the law.

These attitudes are just beginning to emerge in many Middle Eastern Muslim states, and the rates of change are uneven in the various countries. However, on the matter of family planning, there has not been the resistance and social turbulence that has been witnessed in many

Western nations, driven by a theological interpretation that life begins at conception and that reproduction is a legitimate matter for the state.

Economic Pressures on the Family

Despite rapid and massive urbanization in the Arab and Muslim worlds, much of traditional family structure still remains intact. However, some cracks in the foundation of social life are becoming visible. Although the majority of people in the Middle Eastern nations now live in cities, the integrity of the extended family has generally been upheld. Elsewhere urbanization has had a devastating effect on the extended family, and it is likely to have profound effects on the Muslim extended family in the Middle East in the future. In other regions the nuclear family has come to replace the extended family, and in other places the nuclear family has broken down into matrifocal units. Despite massive rural to urban migration and male outmigration from poorer Arab and Muslim nations to richer ones, the essential qualities of the extended family have held together. That is, family members speak of the larger extended family as a unit experiencing either good or bad times, and poor economies at home have brought about a necessary alliance between family members.

However, this is in the short term; in the long term the extended family may not fare so well in the absence of physical unity to reinforce the ideology of family solidarity. In each of the three countries where I have conducted studies of Islamic family law, one of the major areas of concern is the failure of husbands/fathers who have migrated abroad for work to provide adequate economic support to those whom he is bound legally to support. Primarily, this affects the immediate nuclear family, and the majority of court cases have been suits brought by wives against husbands. But with most people still residing in some form of a communal-extended household, the impact is greater than on the nuclear family alone. These changes in the stability of family life may lead to even greater problems if present trends continue, especially if the economic imbalances in the region continue to foster massive rural to urban migration and expatriate migration from the poorer to the richer Arab-Muslim nations.

7

Contemporary Islamic Communities: Tensions from Within and Without

Muslim nations and peoples began the twentieth century as colonial entities and ended it as independent nations, in most cases not yet secure economically or stable politically. Muslim peoples live between the competing cultural traditions of the West, learned through colonialism and defined as modern, and their indigenous heritage, Arabic and Muslim, which was devalued in colonial times. Muslims are engaged in the reclamation and restoration of that heritage, as well as in the modernization of it. The modern Arab world is defined by the tensions between the secularism that was promoted by colonialism (especially the secular politics that grew into Arab nationalism) and the fundamentalism of the Islamic revival (as politicized by the fundamentalists). Moreover, there is a challenge to reformulate Arab society and Muslim culture under the powerful global principles of democracy and human rights. These competing traditions, Western and Eastern, secular and religious, with their economic and political ramifications, comprise the major tensions in Islamic communities today, from without and within.

The Colonial Legacy and Definitions of What is "Modern"

The most important part of the colonial legacy in the Middle East are the nation-states themselves, which were created in their modern form by the European occupiers, either British or French. In a number of cases, such as Egypt, the Sudan, Syria, and Lebanon, the states were created out of the remnants of the Ottoman Empire; in other places, for example, in Kuwait, Saudi Arabia, and other Arabian Gulf nations, they were created de nova. Indigenous nationalist movements were built upon the presumption that the nation-states, as defined, would continue, and there was little talk at the time of independence about the return to precolonial borders or territories. In fact, Saddam Hussein attempted to legitimize his claim to territory in Kuwait on the basis of colonial boundaries drawn by the British. Certainly both sides in the ongoing civil war in the Sudan would agree that the British policy of divide and rule between north and south Sudan exacerbated already hostile feelings left over from Turco-Egyptian rule and the slave trade.

The legacy of colonialism is usually thought of as negative. However, imperial control introduced to the colonies a number of basic institutions of government, law, education, and administration that are still the mainstay of the postindependence nations. For the first several decades after independence, in many countries these basic institutions remained intact, except that they came under local control. Even the transition to the use of Arabic as the official language of government was often delayed due to the dependence on the former colonial structures and procedures. Arabization was accomplished more slowly than the simpler personnel changes from European to indigenous control of offices and schools. In some contexts, such as in the Maghrib countries of Tunisia, Algeria, and Morocco, the use of French as the language of education and cultivation has continued to the present time, with its defenders arguing that literacy in French opens the student-intellectual to a wider world than does the Arabic language. In the Sudan, the Arabization of the curriculum at the University of Khartoum was accomplished only under the Islamist regime in power since 1989, despite earlier interest in this transformation.

The colonial legacy persisted in more subtle cultural ways than language alone, in the cultural values conveyed by language. The colonialist paradigm of cultural superiority is a deeply entrenched belief in the mind of the colonizer, and also of the colonized. Perhaps this is the most difficult part of the colonial legacy to excise. During the decades of colonialism, the standard of the highest achievement in education and politics was to emulate the British or French ways of speaking, thinking and acting; the postcolonial shift to an indigenous set of values created a tension in society, especially along class lines. Upper-class nationals continued to send their children, especially sons, outside of the country for their education or to local institutions that continued to operate in the European fashion. Families that were not so well off sent their children to local schools, where the language of instruction was Arabic and where they were socialized to think that their children were receiving an inferior education.

Outwardly, styles of dress and use of language became highly indicative markers of what Franz Fanon would have called "the interior colonization of mind." It is not uncommon today to overhear two educated Tunisians, fashionably dressed in European suits, conversing in French. It is a sign of their education and breeding. French has so overtaken Tunisian literary culture that contemporary writers, dealing with themes of culture and the colonial legacy, write about the subject more passionately in French than in Arabic. Indeed, their formal education has abjured the use of Arabic, which was seen historically as limited to religious subjects.

In the Levantine countries of Syria and Lebanon, also colonized by France, the impact on local culture was perhaps not as profound as in the Maghrib. But the standard of education for elites certainly included extensive involvement in the French language. Quite remarkably, in Egypt, occupied by France for only a brief period under Napoleon, the legacy of that encounter was the introduction of the Napoleonic code and the basics of French law, as well as an educational and cultural foundation in French which persisted through the subsequent nineteenth and twentieth centuries of British colonialism. The cream of Egyptian elites up to the present are fluent not only in English but also in French.

The attitude of the colonial governments to the religion of Islam and its indigenous institutions was one of cautious respect but firm control. In some instances, where resistance was mounted against foreign control in the name of religion, like the Mahdi of Sudan, military suppression was coupled with a high degree of formal autonomy afforded to Muslim structures and leaders. Independent "Mohammedan" courts were established as a separate judicial entity, with its own court of appeals, but the final authority always rested with the colonial government. The religious establishment may have done little to criticize or oppose colonialism, but religious opposition to foreign domination did develop in political organizations, such as the Muslim Brotherhood, organized in Egypt during colonial times under the leadership of Hasan al-Banna. Their position on Islam was noncompromising and antireformist: Islam is a comprehensive system of religious thought and practice that is sufficient unto itself to solve every political and social problem. They opposed Western imperialism on the grounds that it circumscribed or denied Islam its full place; as such they represented a minority but an important voice in the struggle against colonialism.

The colonial governments were able both to recognize and control the powerful yet competing legacy of the Islamic heritage by appointing their own guardians of that tradition. The state-appointed 'Ulamā' during colonial times were called upon to confirm policies and legal changes that suited their political goals. The end of the practice of child betrothal, the so-called modernization and regulation of waqf and charitable trusts, and other changes regarded as reforms of an archaic system were accomplished by appropriate religious interpretations, fatwas, issued by these 'Ulamā'. To be fair, there is evidence of both restraint on the part of the colonizers and resistance by Muslims and the 'Ulamā' themselves on certain points of religious and social principles. The restraint is explainable in terms of the colonizer's desire not to alienate further a subjugated populace with unpopular reforms. Polygyny, for example, which was disdained by the Europeans on religious and cultural grounds, was not a target of reform. Female circumcision was outlawed in the Sudan in 1946 by the English on religious, medical, and social grounds. However, despite a fatwa that described infibulation as mutilation and therefore forbidden in Islam (Fluehr-Lobban 1987: 97), the practice has continued to the present, although it has been modified by some contemporary midwives (Kenyon 1991). In virtually every colonial situation, both holy days for Muslims and Christians (Friday and Sunday) were observed, and the annual Muslim religious holidays were respected.

The religious leaders who were appointed by the colonial state were, generally speaking, neither controversial nor opposed during their time of government service. However, during the postcolonial secular rule by indigenous officials, their alleged role as apologists for state policy became more apparent. A great deal of credibility was lost by the Grand Mufti and Sheikh of Al-Azhar during the time of Gamal Abdel Nasser's secular, Arab socialist rule in Egypt, when government policy was routinely sanctioned by the 'Ulamā' on a range of subjects from legal reform to foreign affairs. At the same time, the Nasser regime was cracking down on the Muslim Brotherhood, so the impression was given that the highest religious authorities were, in fact, acting on behalf of the government's interests and against Islamic causes.

The antagonistic relationship between the state and resurgent Islam is not new, and the beginning of the distrust of state-appointed 'Ulamā' by Islamic activists is traceable to this early period of independence. This tension within various Islamic societies has sharpened over the decades since independence to the point that some contemporary Islamist activists openly condemn their official religious leadership and seek alternative guidance from more populist sheikhs and imāms. From a perspective that is grounded in the twentieth-century development of Islamic society, this is an utterly modern phenomenon in that the relationship between the state and religion is being questioned in a fundamental way. Ideally, religion and the state are merged in the perfect Islamic society, and religion is not subordinated to the state's interests. Likewise, calls for the restoration of Arabic-language education with Islamic and Arabic studies and for the restoration of Sharī'a to a more central place in the rule of law in state government are viewed as modern demands.

The Proper Contemporary Role for Women

The contradiction between modernity and Islam has been raised in the West. Modernity, after all, is generally equated with westernization rather than with simply being up-to-date. The developments taking place in the Arab-Muslim world may not be viewed as "modern" by the West, but they are certainly very current. Muslim women are confronting conflicting definitions of what it is to be modern. The older secular models derived basically from European colonial contact are being challenged by alternative Islamic ideas in dress, aspiration, and behavior. This is a tension that is felt sharply in contemporary Islamic society, and behavior is increasingly dependent on Islamic interpretations of the proper role for women.

There are certain continuities and discontinuities between the end of colonialism, early independence, and the contemporary period. Education was established as a societal goal later for women than for men in most formerly colonial situations. However, once established, education for women and girls became firmly embedded as a natural right and an expectation for the state to provide. Except for the poorest, most isolated locales, or for those that are experiencing political disruption, as in the Sudan or Palestine, education for girls is normal at least up to the middle school or secondary level. Female literacy is promoted through development programs as well, at least so a young woman can read and understand her marriage contract or a newspaper.

This goal of the support and promotion of female education has not been reduced in the current period of Islamic revival. If anything, it is a twentieth-century trend that has been reinforced through a reinvigorated Islam. Because Islam encourages literacy in order to read and recite the Qur'ān, it follows that a revived Islam will endeavor to bring about a return to reading and studying the Qur'ān. This is exactly what is happening, but what is remarkable is that it includes study groups comprised of and led by women, especially in some of the clandestine Islamist movements in Egypt and Tunisia. This is an entirely new phenomenon. In the past, most khalwas or kuttabs (Muslim schools) were almost exclusively devoted to boys' education. Today education, including religious education, is stressed for both sexes to the highest level attainable. Indeed, the highly motivated young men and women activists involved with contemporary Islamist agitation are drawn from these highly educated segments of society.

While education for women is certainly encouraged, the goals of that education have changed from the goals articulated by the generation of the newly independent states. Female education then stressed career training, while the Islamists argue that the education of women enhances their "natural" roles as mothers and educators. Paradoxically, many of the women Islamist leaders are themselves professional women, such as doctors, lawyers, and university professors. During the recent period of intense Islamist political agitation and influence, the number of women formally entering the work force has increased in countries such as Iran and Egypt.

Education and employment lead to a major dilemma for the Muslim woman: how can she be both Muslim and modern at the same time? The dilemma has been successfully resolved by a large number of Muslim women intellectuals. They have chosen to work outside of the home for wages primarily for one of the same reasons that women in the West have done so: her income is a necessary or a welcome addition to the household. However, leaving the protection of the home for many hours a day, moving about in crowded streets or public transportation, and perhaps having male coworkers are all situations that place a woman in jeopardy, according to traditional Islamic values. Before colonialism and the introduction of Western styles of dress, women typically donned some type of outer covering, known in various cultural contexts as milaya, chador, or thobe, when they left the confines of the home and extended family to go out to visit or shop. This was and continues to be a means of providing modesty and offering protection from the unwanted gazes or physical jostling of strange men in public areas. In a few cases, particularly in the Arabian Peninsula, veiling of the face was also customary.

Women have revived and modernized forms of Islamic-inspired dress as a solution to the conflict implicit in working or studying outside of the home. These are no longer simple sheet-like pieces of material to cover the body, but fashionable long skirts, long-sleeved blouses, and coverings for the head that both conceal the hair and flatter the contours of the face. Cosmetics are not usually worn by the modern woman dressed in this Shar'i way, inspired by Islamic teachings. This type of dress is called *ḥijāb* (meaning "covered" or "protected"). Typically, these are homemade ensembles that are cost-efficient and involve collaborative sharing of patterns, sewing machines, and labor by women. The ḥijāb has become a symbol of revived Islam, and unobtrusive observers may attempt to gauge the depth or popularity of Islamist movements in a country by the number of women seen in public dressed in this way. In some countries where Islamic movements represent a threat to the government, such as *al-Nahḍa* in Tunisia, women dressed in the ḥijāb are harassed on the streets by public security agents. In other countries where the government has cracked down on radical Islamist movements but has adopted a laissez-faire attitude toward wearing of the ḥijāb by women, such as in Egypt, the growth of wearing of some form of ḥijāb has been dramatic and marked. Studies of the adopting of this mode of dress indicate that women have taken to this cultural-religious expression because of its authenticity and congruence with national heritage, because of its practicality and simplicity, and because of its religious meaning. Also mentioned is the growing social pressure of so many women making the change. Wearing the ḥijāb can also have its contextual usage. One woman with whom we were acquainted in Tunis wore the ḥijāb when she was working at an open desk with direct contact with the public but removed her head covering when she worked behind an enclosure.

Likewise, the attitude of many modern Muslim women toward social and legal reform is similarly complex. Some of the legal reforms that

Egyptian women wearing dress that is both modern and Islamic.

offered women emancipation in the wake of the successful independence movements are viewed as Western-inspired changes that are more cosmetic and symbolic than real in terms of women's rights. Egypt's progressive Law 44, inspired by Mrs. Sādāt, is a case in point. The debate over this law revealed the tension between the secular feminists of Egypt's early postindependence period, who perhaps sought change in the status of women more along the lines of the Western woman, and the contemporary Islamic feminists are seeking greater restoration of the traditional Sharīʿa or change in the laws affecting the status of women that conforms to Islamic principles.

Restriction of or the outright elimination of polygyny has probably been the most controversial change proposed by secularists and feminists, who have sought to remove this allegedly archaic remnant of an older Islamic society. Since there is widespread consensus among the 'Ulamāʾ internationally that polygyny is explicitly allowed in the Qurʾān, its removal represents to most Islamists a denial of the truth and validity of the word of God. This principle is defended by the Islamists more so than a steadfast defense of the practice of polygyny. In fact, few Muslim men practice polygyny today.

The right of the wife to adequate support (nafaqa) when her husband is away, during divorce proceedings while they are still legally married, and in certain cases for a period of time after a final divorce has been strongly defended as correct and appropriate in Islamic terms. And the right of the wife to seek judicial divorce has not been challenged by the Islamists, although the social conditions that drive a woman to seek divorce are often criticized.

The degree of personal freedom that a woman or wife should be able to exercise represents another source of tension within contemporary Islamic society. Under traditional Muslim thought and practice, a woman lives under the protection and guardianship of her father and then of her husband. This conforms to patriarchal ideas found in other Western and East Asian societies. However, twentieth-century life has brought many changes that have physically and psychically freed women from traditional bonds. Women move about more openly to carry out errands and household tasks if they are housewives, and increasing numbers of women are working outside of the home. An Islamist view would argue for women working outside of the home in "appropriate" jobs, such as female physicians working at mother-child clinics in pediatric or obstetrical-gynecological medicine. Likewise, an approved type of work for a woman lawyer is a practice focusing on the personal status laws affecting women, such as divorce, child custody, or support cases, and serving primarily female clients.

Some of the stricter Islamists believe that a woman should remain at home after marriage and the birth of children and that a woman seeking employment outside of the home should obtain permission from her husband, father, or guardian. Likewise these so-called fundamentalists want women to obtain permission from their male guardians to acquire a passport or to travel outside of their countries. The Islamist regime in Sudan has invoked this idea to prevent academic women who are critical of the government from traveling abroad, while they have also removed a number of women government employees who are not aligned with the regime, using the Islamic rationale as a justification. Critics of the Islamist approach and human rights activists have opposed this strict and harsh interpretation that limits the freedom and mobility of women.

Rather than signaling an end to women's participation in society and politics, the Islamist upsurge has provided a continuing outlet for women's involvement in the issues of the day. The positive response from women that has been witnessed in the current wave of Islamist activity I see as a continuation of their mobilization and participation in the nationalist movement a generation or more ago. The model and inspiration that the nationalist and feminist women provided have laid the foundation for the Islamist women, some of whom would describe themselves as "Islamic feminists." And why not, since much of the energy that has been generated by the movement has focused on the study and examination of the sources of the religion, the Qur'ān and Sunna, from the perspective of the proper role of women in society, and this has its own liberating and emancipating dimension. Egyptian Muslim feminist Aisha Abdel Rahman argues that the "truly Islamic" and "truly feminist" option is neither immodest dress nor identical roles for men and women in the name of modernity; neither is it sexual segregation and the seclusion of women in the name of Islam. The right path is the one that combines modesty, responsibility, and the integration of women into public life, while honoring the Qur'ānic and naturally enjoined distinctions between the sexes (Hoffman-Ladd 1987: 37).

Some Western observers and Arab and Muslim secularists are deeply concerned about the future status of women under Islamist regimes, insofar as the examples that have emerged in Iran, Saudi Arabia, and the Sudan are not encouraging on this question. On balance, it should be pointed out that dramatic progress in the area of women's rights was not achieved under secular regimes since independence and that the greatest advances have been made when women have agitated on their own behalf with their social and political agenda in hand. There is not much reason to think that an enlightened Islamist government would be any worse than a secular regime, and it might do a better job if it incorporated activist women into the apparatus and policy-making realms of government. As yet, we have not seen this kind of commitment to the inclusion of women by any secular or religious government in the Arab or Muslim world. But we have not yet witnessed this in any Western governments either.

Islamic Revival as a Challenge to the State and Official Islam

So much has been written about the phenomenon of Islamic revival that it is difficult to say something new. Much of the popular discourse in the West on the subject has used the term *Islamic fundamentalism,* perhaps employing the term *fundamentalist* as it is commonly used in the West to describe Christian movements that seek to return to literal interpretations of the Bible and a basic Christian life-style that has been eroded by secularism. In some ways this is a fruitful comparison. However, few Arab or Muslim writers use the term, arguing that among Muslims there is no disagreement about the fundamentals (*usūl*) of the religion, which is based on the holy sources of Qur'ān and Sunna. Thus the Arabic translation of the word *fundamentalism, usūliyya,* conveys little of the meaning and context in English. Likewise, the tendency to lump all of the various Islamist movements under a single, simplifying term is misleading and, ultimately, confusing.

Islamic revival movements have burst on the scene among Shī'a and Sunni Muslims alike, and they have grown in response to decadent kings, such as the shah of Iran; in reaction to military secular regimes, as in Egypt; in single-party secular regimes, as in Tunisia and Algeria; and in irridentist movements weary of the promises of Arab nationalism, such as the Palestinian movement. These historical contexts are too varied to be treated as a single phenomenon, so we struggle to find more appropriate terms that the reader will find here and elsewhere, such as Islamic revival, resurgent Islam, political Islam, or Islamist. The terms that the Islamic activists are using themselves refer to "the call" (*ad-da'wa*), to Islamic renewal and renaissance (al-Nahda), and new dawn, and they are finding ways to live that conform to the teachings of Islam and the Sharī'a. The slogan *Islām huwa al-hāl,* ("Islam is the solution") summarizes and defines their approach.

To the Western politician, preoccupied with the uninterrupted flow of oil from the Middle East and Persian Gulf or the preservation of the status quo in Israel, the threat of Islamic revival and its mass appeal are very much a cause of concern. Some conservative Western observers have voiced concern that, with the end of the cold war, the communist threat will be replaced by the Islamic threat. This point of view has been effectively challenged by an important scholar of Islamic movements, John Esposito, who argues that this view is xenophobic and based on ill-informed and often racist stereotypes of Muslims and Arabs (1992). This expressed fear results more from an ignorance of Islamist movements than the anger and impotence we felt at the time of the Iranian-American hostage crisis. Westerners are still largely ignorant of the religion of Islam and Muslims, yet we seem to feel very comfortable in speaking about the "dangers" of Islamic revival and the backwardness that will ensue and the darkness that will descend upon nations and peoples who follow this path.

To the disenfranchised and unempowered young Muslim in the Middle East or Islamic worlds, a resurgent Islam represents something quite different. It means the possibility of unified action of a more broadly based, mass character than the military or monarchical regimes which have ruled in the name of the people but which are fundamentally undemocratic. The appeal of Islamic revival is that it draws from a rich and powerful religious heritage to challenge the ideologies of Arab nationalism and socialism that have dominated the political arena since the advent of independence.

Certain of these regimes have used the promise of socialism with a distinctly Arab or Islamic character to offer their citizens the hope of economic development and prosperity at home while confronting the Zionist and imperialist ambitions of Israel and the West on the international front. The Arab Socialist Union of Nasser's Egypt, put into power and kept in power by the military, provided the inspiration and the model for a number of sincere imitators. Colonel Muammar Qaddafi of Libya and General Ja'afar al-Numayri of Sudan both seized power in 1969 with movements inspired by Nasser, just two years after the 1967 Six-Days' War and the humiliating defeat of Egypt and of the other Arab states invaded by Israel. In retrospect, it is clear that the 1967 war was the beginning of the end of the confidence of the masses of people in the idea of Arab nationalism, for it brutally revealed that neither the Arab states invaded nor a wider Arab nationalist solidarity could salvage any measure of military or political victory out of this crippling defeat.

On the domestic front the socialist regimes whose political rhetoric emphasized the central role of "the people," the masses (al-Shaʻb) were becoming elitist, personally corrupt, and more withdrawn from the needs of the rural peasantry and urban working classes. The word *al-Shaʻb* became a shopworn, hackneyed political term that over the years lost its legitimacy for mobilizing anything but contempt among the masses. In fact, the term had become so closely associated with Arab nationalist and socialist ideology that an early opposition group to Sādāt, wishing to promote a more genuine Arab socialism, deliberately chose another word that would convey a sense of people's solidarity without the stigma of al-Shaʻb, a point made to me by Hasan Hanafi, the reformist Muslim philosopher, during an interview in Cairo in July 1978. They chose *al-ahāli* as the name for their newspaper and signal term for their movement, a term which carries with it a sense of kindred and close family ties.

Arab nationalism and Islamic enfranchisement continue to drive Islamic revival. To a lesser extent Islamist movements derive their energy from anti-Western sentiments. However, when the content of the many Islamist movements is examined closely, their grievances are focused on their own leaders and their failures; criticism of the West, when it occurs, is often made because of its alliance and support of the leaders in power. This support of unpopular and undemocratic leaders by the West is frequently viewed as an extension of colonialism and evidence of the continuing undue influence of the West upon the Middle East.

The perceived failures of secular Arab nationalist regimes on both the international and domestic fronts have provided a large measure of the fuel for the fires of Islamic renewal. At the same time, the Iranian Islamic Revolution in 1979 made real the dream of a renewed Islam and an Islamic solution to the problems of Muslims and Arabs. Whatever its weaknesses, and many are recognized by other Islamist leaders and followers, the Islamic revolution made possible the rebirth of the idea of Islamic government in the modern era. Within Islamic and Arab societies there is a division in popular attitudes toward the Iranian revolution and, indeed, toward the idea and practice of Islamic revival itself. The committed secularists and Islamists have divergent points of view, but for the majority of people who are neutral or less overtly political there is confusion as to the correct path to follow toward economic development, peace, and the good society. Many people believe that the

Arab nationalists and secularists have had their chance and have failed, so it is timely and appropriate to give the Islamic alternative an opportunity. Others are genuinely fearful when evaluating the current examples of Islamic republics in the world, such as Saudi Arabia, Iran, and the Sudan. Serious questions about the rights of women and non-Muslim minorities have been raised without satisfactory answers in practice.

When the Iranian Islamic revolution occurred, there were demonstrations in support of it throughout the Shī'a and Sunni Muslim worlds, showing that its force was not felt along lines that might be characterized as sectarian. Some Western analysts attempted to comprehend this militancy in Iran in the context of the suffering and veneration of martyrdom that are a part of the observance of Shī'a Islam. However, when similar sentiments were expressed by militant Islamic movements in the Sunni Muslim countries of Egypt, Algeria, Tunisia, the Sudan, and even in the Palestinian movement, historically dominated by Arab nationalist politics, alternative explanations had to be sought. The dramatic growth and influence of the Islamic alternative quickly became a force with which secular nationalist governments had to contend. Hosni Mubarak, taking the lesson from the assassination of Anwar al-Sādāt by a radical Islamic movement, legalized Islamist political parties and allowed them to run for office (they quickly earned 20 percent of the seats in parliament). In Tunisia, Bourgiba's successor, Zein Abdine Ben-Ali, moved to legalize the Islamic Tendency Movement (MTI) when it transformed itself to a political party, al-Nahḍa, and then delegitimized the party, charging that members engaged in violence and proposed the overthrow of the government. Even Saddam Hussein, leader of the historically secular Ba'th Party in Iraq, employed the rhetoric of Islamic jihād, holy war, against the Western allied attackers in the Gulf War and changed the Iraqi flag to read *Allahu Akbar* ("God is almighty") as a cooptation of the strength of the Islamist sentiment. Remarkably, there has not been, as yet, a strong Islamist challenge to the regime of Saddam Hussein, but one directed against his fellow Ba'thist, President Hafez al-Asad of Syria, was crushed.

There is also tension within Muslim society between popular Islam and its new socioreligious organizations and official, state-supported Islam, with its government institutions established to speak for religion. The state-appointed 'Ulamā' have played a difficult and at times ambiguous role during the colonial and postindependence period. As officially anointed guardians of the religion, they defended religious principles against the perceived encroachment of Western ideas and practice contrary to Islam, all the while beholden to the colonial government that employed them. Their work and position could not have been easy, and they surely stood their ground on issues of fundamental interpretation, such as the protection of polygyny, defense of the inheritance laws, and protection of the waqf system. From my own work on Islamic law in the Sudan, it is clear that there was an uneasy relationship between the colonial government's legal secretary, the final legal authority before the governor-general, and the Sharī'a Grand Qadi, first among the government's appointed 'Ulamā' (Fluehr-Lobban 1987).

They differed on many points and the colonial government's effort to impose certain solutions to social and religious problems often met with resistance from these special government employees. Such a case involved the return by force of recalcitrant wives (*bayt al-tā'a*), which the English objected to on practical and moral grounds. Wives repeatedly ran away, and judges were enforcing decrees of "obedience" on the same wife many times. Second, the English thought, why force a woman against her will to remain with a husband she obviously wants to be free of? The 'Ulamā' countered that until the wife was legally divorced according to the rules of Sharī'a, she must continue to obey her husband by returning to his house and living with him, even if this must be accomplished by force. The ideological battle was waged for a number of years until a compromise was reached whereby the order of obedience would be imposed but no more than three times on the same woman. (This element of force has been removed since independence in every country where it was practiced.)

The 'Ulamā', whether in the Sudan or Egypt, with its grand tradition of religious education and scholarship at Al-Azhar University, always publicly pledged their support to the colonial governments, but they surely waged many private struggles that as yet are not fully appreciated or documented. The public appearance was one of accommodation and acceptance of foreign, non-Muslim rule, while the struggles to end foreign rule were carried out by secular nationalists and antistate religious organizations, such as the Muslim Brotherhood. Once independence was won, this gave greater legitimacy to the popular nationalist movements, while the state 'Ulamā' were peripheral to these events. And although they did not lose their authoritative status, because they were and are still seen as religious men, they lost their pivotal role in the achievement of independence.

To a certain extent the sheikhs at the premier Al-Azhar Islamic University have seen themselves as conservators of a religious tradition of interpretation that has survived by not incorporating new ideas. I was invited to meet with some of the scholar-educators on the Law Faculty at Al-Azhar in 1983, while I was living in Cairo and conducting research on family law issues in Egypt. Before entering the university grounds I was asked to cover my head, so I obliged by purchasing a head scarf at a nearby store. As our meeting convened in the office of the chairman of the personal status law division, I was at once awed by being invited to this historic institution and acutely aware of being a non-Muslim, Western woman studying Islamic law. An oddity to them, no doubt, I was nevertheless graciously and respectfully received as one with some background in Islamic legal studies, although my having studied with the Sudanese Grand Qadi did not seem to impress them much. We began discussing family law issues, especially my interest in the divorce law as interpreted and applied in Egypt. Our discussion in Arabic was progressing well, I thought, although they seemed amused by my Sudanese accent in Arabic.

While discussing the gradual elimination of bayt al-ṭāʿa, I was searching for a word in Arabic that conveyed development or change in the law, and I mistakenly, and unfortunately, used the word *taṭwīr*, roughly translated "evolution." I had just been reading some of the works of Islamic reformers in the Sudan, the Republican Brothers, who use the notion of evolution of Islamic institutions such as the law liberally in their writings. I should have used the word for change, *ghayaar*, or some other more neutral term than the inflammatory "evolution," which denies or modifies the essential immutability of the Sharīʿa upon which the conservative religious community relies. Having made my mistake, and having been corrected by the admonition that the Sharīʿa "does not evolve," I felt my interview coming rapidly to a close, and indeed the chairman of the group was the first to excuse himself. Embarrassed by my own unthinking error, I nevertheless gained a valuable perspective on the religious sheikhs at Al-Azhar whose insularity has been a powerful defense.

As secular, Arab nationalist governments came to power and Islamic institutions were seen as interfering with development and "progress," the 'Ulamā' were further isolated and brought under more direct state control. After all, the state was no longer foreign and it became more difficult to oppose it, formally and informally. As mentioned earlier, under Nasser and Sādāt, the Egyptian state-appointed Mufti and Sheikh of al-Azhar were little more than rubber stamps for the government's policies and programs. It has been only the growing strength of the Islamist movement that has emboldened some 'Ulamā' under Mubarak to speak out and oppose government ideas and acts. Some of the more heated battles have occurred in the attempted reform of the personal status laws regarding marriage and divorce, where the more conservative religious scholars have forestalled efforts to restrict polygyny and have upheld the husband's right to divorce without a court order. As a result of these struggles with the government, the 'Ulamā' have regained some of their credibility and thus their capacity to influence the masses of Egyptians who have turned to Islamist alternatives.

In Tunisia, where secular politics still dominate but where the increasingly popular Islamist al-Nahḍa movement has challenged the existing order, the role that the 'Ulamā' historically played under colonialism and under the secular reformist Bourgība has changed little. The state-supported 'Ulamā' are viewed by the Islamists as a part of the same problem to be resolved in the struggle to restore freedom and democracy. Most telling is the fact that the leader of the al-Nahḍa Party, Rachid Ghannouchi, is not from the class of 'Ulamā' but rather was born into a rural farming family and was taught the Qur'ān by his father. His early education was along the lines of the traditional kuttab, but he went on to study philosophy at the Sorbonne and began his professional life as a teacher. Only one of the other leaders of the Islamic movement, Sheikh Abdel Fattah Mourou, could be described as coming from the 'Ulamā'. Some of the religious sheikhs, whose influence has been curtailed by the state, meet privately with their followers to counsel them. While in Tunis, I learned of several cases of Muslims disaffected by the government's alienation from Islam. These people chose to seek the clandestine advice of such sheikhs, preferring them to the use of the Tunisian official legal system.

In countries that have undergone a progressive political Islamization over the past two decades, as in the Sudan, the traditional 'Ulamā' were bypassed in favor of former Muslim Brotherhood leader Hasan al-Turābi, who was made attorney-general under President al-Numayri. During his time in office he oversaw the introduction of Sharī'a law as state law in 1983. The Muslim Brotherhood in Sudan, reborn as the National Islamic Front in 1985, came to power in 1989 and has steadfastly opposed any efforts to rescind the executive order making Islamic law state law, despite the fact that it is a central issue in the chronic civil war between north and south Sudan.

The tension between the traditional 'Ulamā' and the leadership of the various Islamist movements is palpable. Although the 'Ulamā' can still command respect for their religious knowledge, if not their political alliances, the new Islamist leaders are self-taught and rely on the purity of the sources themselves and encourage independent collective study of the Qur'an, Sunna, and Hadīth; they also encourage study circles comprised of women only. This undermines the monopoly on knowledge and interpretation that the 'Ulamā' once held and represents a dramatic democratization of access to and use of religious knowledge, with wideranging implications.

Islam, Democracy, and Human Rights

The greatest political challenge to the range of movements we in the West have called Islamic fundamentalism is the accusation that Islamic movements, when they come to power, are undemocratic and weak in the application of basic human rights, especially with regard to women and non-Muslims living in Islamic republics. This sentiment is so profound that, when a preemptive coup stopped the Islamists who had won the national election in Algeria early in 1992, hardly a complaint was heard in Western editorial pages. What is to follow is not an apology for Islamist regimes currently in power but an exploration of the ideas and concepts by which the West judges the Middle East.

Notions of human rights and democracy are rooted in Western history. The concept of human rights has been a clarion call to those struggling for freedom from oppression in Western settings, such as in the American colonies and the first black republic of Haiti. Since the creation of the United Nations, the upholding of basic human rights, outlined in its Universal Declaration of Human Rights, has been a part of the international agenda. In the United States the administration of

President Jimmy Carter placed human rights on the national agenda. Today it is a key concept by which nations and their actions are judged.

In the Islamic world two separate tendencies are present with respect to human rights, *al-huqūq al-insān*. The first is a liberal view that argues that the essential ideas of Islamic thought and practice, properly interpreted, are fully compatible with democracy and international standards of human rights. The second is an Islamist view that places first priority on a religious foundation for the state that is essentially communitarian (based on the idea of Umma), where a just social order will necessarily emerge from the proper application of Islamic principles (Sisk 1992: viii).

The liberal tradition can be traced to the writings of the great Egyptian jurist Muhammad Abduh and the advocate of women's rights Qasim Amin, both of whose writings had an impact in the region around the turn of the century. One of its leading contemporary exponents is Said al-Ashmawy, also a noted jurist and outspoken critic of those he calls the Islamic "extremists," who has been interviewed widely in the Western media, in both French and English language periodicals and newspapers. Al-Ashmawy, a friend and colleague with whom I have collaborated in the past, is currently under twenty-four-hour armed guard due to threats from Islamist radicals. He argues that the Islamists place Islamic rights over human rights (1992: 2). In the liberal interpretation, human rights can never conflict with or contradict Islamic law. Al-Ashmawy points out that of the 6,000 verses in the Qur'ān, only 80 deal specifically with legal rules; the remainder of what is Islamic law is developed by humans and not part of revelation. As such, rules are subject to discussion, debate, and change within a free and open context, where there is no compulsion or threat of silencing alternative viewpoints. The state, as it has developed in the colonial and postindependence period, is and should be outside of the realm of religion. Politics is neither a pillar nor a fundamental cornerstone of Islam, and as Al-Ashmawy argues, a religious state would be totalitarian because it would give its own acts the quality of divinity and would demand passive and absolute obedience from its subjects (1988–89: 4).

The Islamist view of democracy rests with the principle of *shūra* or consultation, in which the ruler (the caliph or imām) may accept advice from counselors whom he has appointed, although he has no obligation to follow their advice, even if there is consensus among them. An allied concept is *ijma'*, meaning consensus of the legal scholars used in Islamic jurisprudence, which is used to discuss changes in legal interpretation. Such consensus has been achieved regarding Islamic attitudes toward insurance and banking but such matters as polygyny and divorce remain controversial. According to the Islamist leader of the Sudan, Dr. Hasan al-Ṭurābi, shūra and ijmāʿ, used together, form the basis for legitimate Islamic government (1992). Democracy, he points out, is a Western concept developed in a secular context that has been applied to Islamic societies, whose premise is religious. This makes for neither fair nor legitimate comparison, and democracy need not necessarily mean political parties and ballot boxes. Consultation and consensus, in the Islamic model of government, are sufficient to satisfy the requirement of democracy in the Muslim state.

While Western notions of democracy need not be met to satisfy an Islamic concept of right government, in cases where Islamist political parties are achieving greater influence through democratic elections, as in Algeria, Egypt, and Jordan, the clash between Western ideas of secular democracy and Islamist religious agendas is most acute. Western and secular critics of Islamist politics cannot delegitimize the ballot box; democracy, as voiced through people voting directly in elections, is indivisible. Democracy is democracy, even if the outcome is an Islamist regime. The popular election of the Islamists in Algeria in 1991 was highly disturbing and controversial, for many critics of the Islamist approach contended that democracy, for women and for the secular parties, would ultimately be denied by an Islamic republic using democratic means to come to power. Said al-Ashmawy agrees with this view, arguing that any religious state whose rule is based upon the exercise of the "divine will" will necessarily abuse power and justify it on religious grounds (1988–89). This sharp division regarding the ability of Islamic governments to respect and enforce what are basically Western ideas about democracy creates major tension within Islamic societies and between them and the West.

The difference between these two points of view represents the deepest and most serious fissure within contemporary Islamic society. The ideas are mutually exclusive, ideologically and practically, and success of one of these viewpoints means the defeat of the other. In some countries it has become a matter of life and death, and Muslim liberals have been jailed and forced into exile where Islamic republics have suppressed their point of view, such as in Iran and the Sudan, and Said

Al-Ashmawy has lived in constant need of personal protection since 1986 (information from personal communication with Richard Lobban during a visit to Cairo in July 1993). Increasingly, the debate between liberals and Islamists has sharpened to differences over human rights and the right to dissent within an Islamic context.

Human Rights

There exists a rather pessimistic view among some Arab intellectuals that democracy is a luxury of the so-called developed countries and that it is a stage of political maturity that will come only in the future for Arab and Muslim societies. The issue of human rights may be one that hastens that day.

Over the past decade or more the term used to refer to human rights, *al-ḥuqūq al-insān,* has gained a wide currency in the Arabic-speaking Middle East (Dwyer 1991: 8). In terms of formal organization, the Tunisian Human Rights League has a long history, as has the Arab Organization for Human Rights. Other organizations have been formed in the midst of political struggle where basic human rights have been allegedly violated, such as the Sudan Human Rights Organization, founded in the late 1980s. In the period since the Islamists came to power in 1989, they have allied themselves with the secularist opposition National Democratic Alliance (Mahmoud 1992). However, in Tunisia, where government repression of the Islamist al-Nahḍa has been criticized and cited by Amnesty International and the Tunisian Human Rights League, the call for democracy and human rights has been raised by an Islamic group against a secular government. Thus the human rights movement has joined forces with both secular and religious movements for democracy without any apparent contradiction between alleged violations by secular or religious regimes.

In the Sudan the alleged violations include lengthy detentions without charges, absence of due process, summary trials and executions, house arrests, disappearances and torture; denial of free expression, assembly, and movement (including denial of passports and visas); and confiscation of property (Ali 1992). In Tunisia, the list of alleged human rights violations is the same (The Renaissance Party in Tunisia 1991). Some anthropologists have raised the question as to whether human rights is a universal doctrine or a Western idea that has gained currency in the world for political expediency; at least in these two different cases the context appears to be less significant than the common call for democracy and political freedom.

Two of the areas where it has been alleged that Islamic rule denies basic human rights are its dealings with women and with non-Muslim minorities. This weakness has been raised when secular state constitutions weigh in against Islamic ideas about the status of women and the proper governance of non-Muslims in an Islamic state. Many secularly inspired constitutions provide equal rights for all citizens, irrespective of sex or religious affiliation. However, as the call for Islamic government has been heard, strict interpretation of Shari'a provisions regarding women and religious minorities has been enforced by Islamist regimes. This has meant that women and non-Muslims have been excluded from certain political and governmental positions, such as attaining appointment to or continuing in positions as judges. In the Sudan, Tunisia, Iraq, and other states with strong secular feminist movements historically, women have been admitted to positions as judges in both civil and Islamic courts. Egypt has not shared in this tradition, despite its influential feminist movement, and it has followed the more conservative Islamic interpretation that a woman cannot sit in a position of power and authority over a man. Egypt has many women lawyers but no women judges; Tunisia has a high percentage of both. A young woman lawyer has filed suit for the right to become Egypt's first female judge. Fatma Abdel Ra'ouf Lashin has based her case on Egypt's constitution, which emphasizes the principle of equality in all matters affecting its citizens. Even the Islamists and the conservative 'Ulamā' agree that the unofficial ban on female judges has more to do with tradition than with religion. This conservative ban would also logically exclude women from serving as heads of state, but clearly it is not a universal ban since the current prime ministers of Pakistan, Benazir Bhutto, and Turkey, Tansu Cillar, are women.

Other Shari'a restrictions on women that might violate secular constitutional guarantees of equality include the general rule of a half portion of inheritance to which women are entitled under Islamic law and their status as only half-witnesses in court, that is, two women witnesses are the equivalent of one man. This latter rule is applied only where Islamic law is the sole law in force or where it governs personal status affairs; otherwise women are considered full witnesses with men in civil cases. The half portion in inheritance has not been challenged, since it is explicitly mentioned in the Qur'ān and is justified by the injunction

"Men are in charge of women because they spend of their property (for the support of women)" (sūra 4:34). In fairness, men are obliged to support their wives, children, and other immediate family members, such as parents, while women have no such obligation, so the inequity alleged here may not be so great as it first appears.

The position of non-Muslims is similar in that they may be relegated to second-class status under an Islamic government, where they may also be denied the right to govern or hold positions of power over Muslims. The need for protection of the non-Muslim, *dhimmis,* and the historical payment of a special tax for that purpose have been criticized as archaic and in need of reform by modern Islamic societies. The Sudanese Republican Brotherhood, an Islamic reformist movement, specifically rejects this inferior status of non-Muslims, saying that it is incompatible with the modern multicultural and multireligious state. It is likewise critical of the "incorrect" interpretation that makes second-class citizens of women as well, basing its own more liberal interpretation on the holy sources, especially the earlier, more universal texts of the Qur'ān revealed at Mecca (Magnarella 1982).

Southern Sudanese have justifiable fears for their protection as non-Muslims under the current Islamist regime, and past regimes have attempted to solve the problem of non-Muslim status through conversion, coerced Islamization, or political isolation rather than by integration. The current spotlight on human rights abuses in the Sudan has raised important practical questions about the Islamist treatment of women and non-Muslim minorities. Critics charge that it is an abuse of Islam and a misapplication of Sharī'a to force women to cover themselves in certain "religiously correct" ways or to limit their freedom of movement or free exercise of the right to work.

Any perceived or real Islamic limitation of human and civil rights must be addressed within Muslim communities, as they surely are being addressed by critical observers in the West, and by many Muslim secularists who seek to keep religion separate from the state.

Islamic Economics: Contemporary Banking and Finance

The creation of Islamic alternatives in the economic sphere is not well known in the West. The Islamic banking and finance movement was

Islamic bank in Khartoum.

synthesized by a combination of religious philosophy and practical need to meet the economic demands of Muslims engaging in local and international commerce. The Islamic banks were started with capital from the oil-rich Gulf states—Saudi Arabia, Dubai, and Bahrain—and they have continued to play a dominant role in the ownership of these alternative financial institutions. Although the finance capital originates in the Gulf among some of its richest families, for example in the Faisal Islamic banks, most of the Islamic banks have been established in the poorer Arab states—chiefly Egypt, the Sudan, and Jordan—where they have come to dominate smaller local banking needs. It is virtually impossible to separate the movement to promote Islamic economics from the movement to restore Islamic principles in government and society.

The religious inspiration for an Islamic system of economics stems from the Qur'ānic prohibition on usury, *riba,* which in itself derives from the fundamental principle of tawḥīd, the unity and oneness of God, and the relationship of cooperation and equity that is commanded between Muslims. Anything that divides the Muslim community, such as unjust economic practices involved in usury, is forbidden in Islam. The Qur'ān specifically condemns the taking of interest on loans as a form of expropriation, since it claims more from a person's capital than its fair value. Likewise, it is commonly said that it is wrong to profit from another person's hardship, the assumption being that only a needy person seeks a loan.

The Islamic alternatives that have been devised to avoid interest-taking in banking and loans emphasize partnership and profit-sharing in investment over the use of interest-bearing loans. A common type of loan from an Islamic bank is known as *muḍāraba*, whereby the bank loans money to a client to finance a business venture in return for which the bank receives a specified percentage of the net profits of the business for a designated period. Share of the profits provides for repayment of the principle plus a profit for the bank to pass on to its depositors. Should a muḍāraba enterprise lose money or fail to thrive, the bank, the borrower, and the bank's depositors all jointly absorb the loss. This puts into practice the basic Islamic principle that lenders and borrowers of capital should share risks and rewards.

Another commonly used technique is *murābaha*, in which the bank purchases goods in its own name and takes title to these goods, then sells them at an agreed upon mark-up. The profit that the bank derives is justified in terms of the service rendered. This technique is frequently used for the financing of trade.

Trade and commerce must also conform to Islamic teachings. No commercial dealing with alcohol, drugs, pork or pork products, or pornography or any sexually exploitative material is permitted. Some interpretations also ban trade in guns, ammunition, and other weapons that are designed to destroy life; buying or selling these items is forbidden (*harām*).

Islam does not not condemn profit-taking from legitimate businesses as long as the accumulation of wealth is not based on interest earned by loaning money. For example, loans made by the Islamic Development Bank to poorer Islamic countries using capital from the richer Arab-Muslim nations are interest-free. This stands in marked contrast to the interest-bearing loans made by the Western capitalist nations, whose banking systems and economies are founded on loaning money at prescribed interest rates. Poorer nations often use their entire GNP to pay off the interest on loans from Western financial institutions like the World Bank or International Monetary Fund. While loans from the

Islamic Development Bank may have other strings attached that make them less desirable, the element of long-term indebtedness that often characterizes loans from the West is absent.

The Islamic banking movement reflects popular Islamist sentiment and propagandizes for it. In the Sudan the Islamic banking movement is closely tied to the growth of the National Islamic Front and is largely responsible for funding it. Islamic banks, exempted from state regulation, have come to dominate all banking transactions under the current Islamist regime. The banks have offered opportunities to small- and medium-sized business ventures that have aided in their mass appeal, and they have served to break the monopoly of some of the old merchant families that have dominated trade and commerce since colonial times. Because 60 percent of the capital, on average, is foreign based, typically Saudi or other Gulf state money, the stability of the banks depends on the maintenance of good ties with these nations. During the Gulf War the Sudan sided with Iraq and thus incurred the wrath of Saudi Arabia, which then limited its flow of capital into the country. The Sudan then turned to Iran, which has also Islamized its banking system, for economic and military assistance.

Islamic banking and financial institutions have not always lived up to the high standard expected of a religiously based institution. In Egypt, for example, Islamic investment corporations established envious reputations for high rates of return on money invested, sometimes as much as 20–25 percent. These high figures brought greater interest and more capital to the Islamic alternative, not necessarily for religious motives. Standing outside of government regulation, some improprieties were inevitable. In Egypt during the late 1980s there was a scandal involving corruption and misrepresentation of monies invested in several of the largest Islamic investment corporations. The government stepped in and imposed strict guidelines over what had been a laissez-faire and uncontrolled economic situation. There is no doubt that the Egyptian government also sought to exercise some political control over this particular dimension of the Islamic revival movement.

The challenge presented by the existence and dramatic growth of the Islamic banks is one faced by secular regimes that fear these banks' ties to the Islamic revival movements but are reluctant to restrain the banks and their home nations—for fear of popular resistance. The Islamic banks present an indigenous challenge to Western financial institutions, such as the English-based Barclay's Bank or the U.S.-based Citibank, which have been accustomed to controlling the movement of foreign capital in many Arab-Muslim nations; they may find that regional Islamic financial institutions will replace the international flow of capital among Muslim nations.

Likewise, the appeal of an economic system that operates on totally different premises, such as the Islamic ban on interest-taking as a form of usury, has broad appeal for the debt-ridden nations of the world and for poor people in general. For example, I find that many of my students, who are themselves struggling to make ends meet, are attracted to the ideas of Islamic economics. Even the more cynical among them, who see banking fees and service charges as a form of interest taken by the Islamic banks, yield the point that the system is more open to the poorer echelons of society and therefore has popular appeal. Some African-American and other Muslim students point with pride to the economic alternatives that have sprung up within Muslim communities in the United States and North America, whereby mortgages on houses and car loans are made using Islamic principles that bypass the usurious loans made by American banks. These loans involve the joint purchase of the house, for example, by a group of Muslim investors who receive "rent" or "use" payments from the occupant of the home, who is also an investor. When the home is eventually sold and a profit presumably made, all of the investors share in the profit made from the sale. Islamic investment corporations have been established in a number of North American cities to handle these alternative economic transactions for Muslims seeking a banking method that conforms to their religious principles.

In a related vein, Muslims living in North America are advised not to use VISA or MasterCard credit cards because they charge interest rates for the credit they offer. It is, or has been, preferable to choose American Express or some other credit card that charges an annual service fee instead of taking interest on the advance of credit.

To the average American many of these ideas make sense as a collective approach to solving what are otherwise individual financial dilemmas. However, the social collectivity, based in religion or some other common bond, is difficult to create in Western society, which has been erected so fundamentally upon individualism.

Conclusion

Tensions within Islamic communities and nations have sharpened within the past two decades as Islamist political movements have increasingly challenged Arab nationalist and secular regimes. The debates regarding the role of religion in government, the proper conduct and status of women, the definition of democracy, and the protection of human rights are both theoretical and practical. Differences of view engage Muslim and non-Muslim citizens of different states from the Maghrib to northeast Africa and the Middle East. The outcome of this great internal dialogue and struggle is of utmost interest to the Western nations with long-standing economic and political interests in the region. We in the West need to understand the nature of the debate and accept its outcome, even if it is not the most desirable one from the standpoint of our best interests. The Western dilemma that combines a fascination with an avoidance and ignorance of Islamic and Arab culture can be resolved by an openness to that culture, an approach to the culture on its own terms, a recognition that it has strengths and weaknesses as does Western culture. We know that Western culture cannot be understood in all of its complexity by the use of simplistic generalizations, for example, that Westerners are violent, materialistic, or sexually permissive. Arab and Muslim people would, likewise, prefer to be viewed with some objectivity beyond simple stereotyping.

The Islamic religious and cultural system has proven its powerful ability to mobilize people. The legitimacy that this heritage conveys is more than the West can successfully confront or defeat, except militarily. We in the West must learn the issues in the region so that we can communicate better with Arab and Islamic leaders, as well as better represent our own interests. Islamist and secular governments in the Muslim-Arab world will continue to foster dialogue and good relations with the West if we are prepared to come to a forum where both sides are engaged in enlightened, mutually self-interested relations.

This book is offered in the hope that it might make Islamic society and the Middle East region more human, more understandable, and less threatening to the Westerner interested in moving toward a deeper understanding of Arab and Islamic cultures. Even if some Western readers are informed without necessarily gaining a cultural appreciation and increased tolerance for Islamic society, then one purpose of this book will be well served because information will replace ignorance. If greater understanding is achieved, then a more valuable humanistic goal will have been reached.

As we in the West struggle to move beyond a bipolar world, driven for so many years by East-West antagonism between the United States and Western Europe, and the Soviet Bloc, we are envisioning a multi-centered world in which the West is one of several regional centers on an increasingly interdependent globe. The civilizations of the Arab and Muslim peoples and the regions in which they are dominant are surely one center with which we must become better acquainted and with which we will surely contend time and again in the future. If we accept that we have both influenced this cultural region and have been influenced by it, then bilateral understanding can replace unilateral thinking. This means incorporating into our basic education and worldview the idea of a shared Judeo-Christian-Islamic heritage, where both convergent and divergent forces have operated. Such an approach does not weaken the West but strengthens our worldview.

Appendix A

Glossary of Arabic Terms and Names

'Abd—slave or servant, used in Arab names with one of the names of Allah, such as 'Abdallah or 'Abd al-Karim'

'Abīd—enslaved persons, used as a derogatory reference, may mean "blacks" or Africans

al-Ahāli—corporateness as derived from being a part of an extended family

Ahl al-Kitāb/Kitabiyīn—"people of the Book"; reference to Christians and Jews, protected in a Muslim state and eligible as marriage partners for Muslim men

"Ahlan wa Sahlan"—standard Arabic greeting, like "Hello"; from original Arab greeting, "Be at ease, you are safe here."

'Ā'ila—extended family

al-Ajnabi—any foreigner, or outsider; from Arabic root meaning "lateral", or "on the side"

'Alawi sect—Shi'a religious sect

'Alī—son-in-law of Muhammad and fourth caliph, whose rule precipitated a crisis over succession in the caliphate; those siding with 'Alī were known as Shī'at 'Alī or, subsequently, as Shī'a Muslims

'Alim—one who is knowledgeable or learned. See also 'Ulamā'

"Allahu Akbar"—"God is great or almighty"; religious saying often heard in the political context of Islamic revival

'Aqd—Muslim marriage contract signing ceremony

'Arab—one who speaks Arabic as a first language, self-identifies as "Arab"; a collective term for people of Arab descent; also a nomad, Bedouin.

'Asaba—core group of patrilineally related males

Atatūrk, Mustafa Kemal—architect of modern Turkey, who secularized religious institutions, changed the writing of Turkish from Arabic to Roman script and "modernized" Islamic institutions

'Ayb—shameful behavior

Al-Azhar Mosque and Al-Azhar University—the oldest and the premier university of Islamic studies, in Cairo (Jāmi'at al-Azhar)

al-Banna, Hasan—founder of the Muslim Brotherhood in Egypt

Baraka—blessings from God, obtained by performing religious acts

Ba'th Party—"Renaissance" Party of Arab nationalism, especially prominent in Iraq and Syria

Bayt al-ṭāʿa—"house obedience" of the Muslim wife interpreted legally as the obligation to cohabit with her husband

Bint ʿamm—father's brother's daughter, or patrilateral first cousin; the preferred marriage partner

Bourgība, Habīb—first president of independent Tunisia, leader of the nation's secular nationalist Destour Party and reformer of Islamic family law

Dār al-Islām/Dār al-Harb—the "place of peace", where the religion of Islam prevails, as contrasted with the "place of war," where non-Muslims predominate; used in the context of external jihād

Ḍarar—"Harm" to the wife, developed as a legal concept in Mālikī law and used to reform Islamic divorce

Dastur Party—Constitution Party of Tunisian independence movement, led by Habīb Bourgība

Daʿwa—the call to religion that is a part of the contemporary vocabulary of Islamic activists

Dawla—"the state" in the Arabic language, as distinguished from jamhūriya (republic) or individual states (wilayaat) or provinces that are part of a larger nation, as in al-Wilayaat al-Muttahida (the United States)

Dervish—Turkish; Persian referent to Ṣūfī practitioners who may employ whirling in religious performance to produce a religiously ecstatic state; Darwish in Arabic

Dhikr—"remembrance"; Ṣūfī rituals performed in remembrance of God

Dhimmi—non-Muslim in a Muslim state

Dhu al-Hijja—literally, the "one of the pilgrimage," meaning the time of performing the pilgrimage to Mecca

Effendi, Effendum—"Sir", "Madam" in Arabic, especially common in Egypt

"Essalaam alay kum"—"Peace be upon you"; the universal greeting of Muslims

Fallahīn/fellaheen—Arab peasantry at the core of Middle Eastern rural life

Faqīh, Foqahāʿ (pl.)—trained in the sources of the religion; interpreters of the religious law (al-Fiqh)

Faranj—foreigner, often used in reference to Westerners, from the "Franks," the Crusaders

Farsi—language of Persia (contemporary Iran)

Fatwa—a legal opinion that may be formalized by the power of the state

al-Fiqh—Islamic jurisprudence; what the foqahāʿ interpret

al-Gharīb—"foreign," "strange," refers to any stranger; derived from Gharb, meaning "the West"

Hadīth—the collected, written tradition of the sayings and actions of the Prophet Muḥammad

Hajj—pilgrimage to the holy places of Mecca and Medina; one of the five pillars of Islam

"al-Hamdulillah"—"Praise be to God"; a fundamental element of Arabic conversation and worldview

Hanafī—one of four main schools of Islamic jurisprudence

Hanbalī—one of four main schools of Islamic jurisprudence

Harām—"forbidden" in Islam, as the consumption of alcohol or the eating of pork; contrasts with *halāl,* that which is approved

Harīm/Hareem—traditionally, "forbidden" area of the home where women are protected from contact with unrelated men

Hayy/Hai—residential area where neighbors are often relations

Hiba—gift made legal by formal declaration

Hijāb—"covering"; used in reference to Islamic-style dress increasingly adopted by women in the Arab-Islamic world, such as chador, milaya, or thobe; also refers to religious amulets that contain ("cover") sacred texts

Hijāz—traditional Arabic reference to the western shores of the Arabian Peninsula

Hijra—"Flight", "migration"; specifically, the flight of the Prophet and the early community of Muslims from Mecca to Medina in the year 622 C.E., thus marking the first year of the Islamic calendar, reckoning time after the Hijra, A.H. (anno hegirae)

al-Huqūq al-Insān—"human rights"

'Id—religious holiday

'Id al-Adha—Feast of Sacrifice; 'Id al-Kabir, or Great Holiday

'Id al-Fitr—holiday ending the month of fasting, Ramadān

'Idda—period of three monthly courses observed by the wife after the dissolution of marriage due to divorce or death of the husband; ensures the legitimacy and paternity of any possible unborn child

Ihram—white garment worn during the performance of the Hajj

Ijmā'—"consensus" of the legal scholars on an issue of religious interpretation

Ijtihād—legal interpretation of the holy sources, Qur'ān and Sunna

Ikhtilāt—open socializing between men and women, which many Islamists criticize and abjure

'Ilm—knowledge or learning

Imām—a leader of prayer, often used in reference to the leader of a local mosque

Infitāh—"opening"; especially the economic opening of Egypt to the West that characterized the policies of Anwar al-Sādāt

"Inshā' Allāh"—"Godwilling"; an expression that is a basic part of Arabic conversation and worldview

Iqrār—legal acknowledgment of a fact, such as paternity

Islam—The peace that comes from submission to the one God, Allah; the last of the great prophetic traditions traceable to Abraham

Jāhiliyya—the time of ignorance that preceded Islam in the Arabian Peninsula

Jamā'a—group or collective

Jamhūriya—"republic"; used as a designation of various post-independence Arab states which are not monarchies

Jami'—mosque

Jāmi'a—university

al-Jazīra al-Arabīyya—"Arab island"; Arabic reference to the Arabian Peninsula

Appendix A

Jihād—"Struggle" or great effort of Muslims, which can be either internal, as in the struggle within oneself to live an upright life, or external, as in the better-known "holy war" to defend the religion

Jinn—"spirit" or supernatural force; in Arabic folktales, refers to a mythical being endowed with supernatural powers; "genie" in English is derived from *jinn*

Jizya—tax for protection of dhimmis

Ka'ba—sacred enclosure at the center of the Great Mosque in Mecca; the focal point of Muslim prayer

al-Kafa'a fil zawāj—"equality of standard in marriage"; insured by a woman's marriage guardian (al-wali) that she will marry a man whose family background is equivalent to her own in religion, education, and economic standing

Karām—generosity; a basic value in Arab-Islamic society

Karāma—personal dignity, honor

Khalīfa—"caliph"; rightful successor in Islamic state

Khalwa—"retreat" or "secluded place"; Islamic school for learning to read and write the Qur'ān

Khawāja—common term for a foreigner, usually European or of European extraction; colloquial for "mister" in the Levant

Khul'—negotiated divorce by mutual consent; one of the traditonally permitted forms of divorce

Kuttab—Islamic school

Lawh/loh—writing board used in Islamic schools

Madhhab, madhāhib (pl.)—school of Islamic jurisprudence, as in Māliki, Hanafī, Shafi'ī, or Hanbalī

Maghrib—"the West," or place where the sun sets; contemporarily refers to the northwestern African countries of Tunisia, Algeria, and Morocco

Mahdī—an expected deliverer and religious purifier in the Messianic tradition of Judaism, Christianity, and Islam; one who is divinely guided and will come to save humanity; the Sudanese Mahdī, Muhammad Ahmad, is among the best known

Mahr—Islamic dower, without which a legal marriage cannot be contracted; this is a large amount of wealth subject to inflationary increases, which some Islamist activists have rejected by reducing the mahr to a modest or symbolic token of wealth

Maktūb—"that which is written"; can refer to the completion of a marriage contract or a sense of one's fate having been "written"

Māliki—one of four main schools of Islamic jurisprudence

Marabout (Arabic, murābit)—a pious or holy one, a "saint," or one believed to have special abilities to communicate with God; subject to frequent veneration in North African traditions

"Marhaba"—"Welcome"; standard greeting in Arabic and Turkish

Mashriq—"the East"; refers to the eastern Arab countries, such as Egypt or Syria

Masjid—mosque, place of worship; from *sajāda* (prostration)

Mawlid al-Nabi—religious holiday celebrating the birth of the Prophet

Mihrāb—niche in a mosque which indicates the qibla or the direction of Mecca for prayer

Mudāraba—in Islamic law, limited or silent partnership

Mufti—"one who opens the way"; one with legitimate authority to issue an official religious opinion, or fatwa; also the official title of the highest religious leader, as the Mufti of Egypt

Mujāhidīn (m.)/mujāhidāt (f.)—fighters or stalwarts in a holy crusade

Murābaha—in Islamic law, resale with specification of gain

Mut'a—"indemnity"; interpreted in Egypt as a divorce compensation over and above the legal obligation of support (nafaqa)

Muwāthiq—public notary

Nafaqa—maintenance or support legally owed by the husband/father to his wife and children in Muslim marriage

al-Nahda Party—"Awakening", or "Renaissance" Party of Islamic revival in Tunisia

Nasab—genealogy, determined by legitimate birth to a legally married couple; genealogy is reckoned patrilineally through the father's line

Nasser, Gamal Abdel—Arab nationalist leader of Egypt from 1952 until his death in 1969

al-Numayri, Ja'afar—military ruler (president) of the Sudan from 1969 to 1985

Qadi—a judge in an Islamic court

Qarāba—"nearness" or "closeness" in Arabic kinship; describes physically and genealogically close relations within the extended family

Qasīda—an ancient Arab ode, composed to be sung

Qibla—the direction of prayer, toward the Ka'ba in Mecca

Qur'ān—the Holy Book of Islam; the word of God revealed to his messenger, Muhammad

Quraysh—coming from the extended family or lineage of the Prophet

Ramadān—lunar month of fasting (sawm); at the end of Ramadān comes the great holiday, the 'Id al-Fitr, when the fast is broken

Riba—interest-taking on money loaned, usury; forbidden in Islam

al-Sādāt, Anwar—Egyptian military and secular nationalist leader who succeeded Nāsser and opened economic relations with the West and political relations with Israel; he was assassinated in 1981 by a radical Islamist group, *Takfīr wa Hijra* (Deliverance and Flight)

Salāt—prayer, five times a day at specified times; one of the five pillars of Islam

Sawm—fasting during the holy month of Ramadān; one of the five pillars of Islam

al-Sha'b—"the people"; a standard reference in secular nationalist political rhetoric

Shafi'i—one of the four main schools of Islamic jurisprudence

Shahāda—the testament of belief and the most fundamental pillar of Islam; There is no God but Allah, and Muhammad is his Messenger

Sharāf—honor conveyed to a family or individual by upright living within a community; sharīf (m.) or sharīfa (f.)

Shar'i—proper, lawful religious behavior, as interpreted by contemporary Islamists

Sharī'a—"the correct path"; Islamic law as it has been interpreted by the foqahā' belonging to one of the four main schools of Islamic jurisprudence

Shaykh/Sheikh—religious and/or political leader of a group, from the level of a small study circle to a village leader, or university professor

Shī'a Islam—the branch of Islam traced to the historical dispute in the early decades after the introduction of the religion over the question of succession, whether the rightful caliph should be from the family of Alī, the Prophet's son-in-law, or from among the pious Muslims

Shūra—"consultation"; a method approximating democracy by which Islamic rulers should govern

Şūfī—the mystical path in Islam, derived from the Arabic *suf* (wool), garments worn by some Şūfīs and symbolizing a lack of regard for the material world; the Şūfī Way is characterized by the performance of *dhikrs,* rituals which emphasize music and dance and a populist approach to religion

Sunna—practice of the Prophet during his lifetime; one of the ideals of Muslim behavior

Sunni Islam—the majority branch (90 percent) of the world's Muslim population, as contrasted with the minority Shī'a branch of Islam

Suq—Arab marketplace, bazaar

Sūra—verse from the Qur'ān

Ṭa'a—odedience required of a wife, interpreted as cohabitation with her husband

Ṭalāq—divorce

Ṭalāq al-'ayb—divorce due to impotence in the husband

Ṭalāq al-ḍarar—judicial divorce ordered by a Sharī'a judge due to confirmed harm or neglect in the marriage

Ṭalāq Khawf al-fitna—divorce because of fear of temptation, granted to a woman fearing illicit behavior on her part due to the prolonged absence of her husband

Ṭalāq Thalātha/ṭalāq talāta (coll.)—divorce by triple pronouncement, "I divorce you three times"

Ṭarīqa, ṭuruq (pl.)—Şūfī religious brotherhoods

Ṭaṭwīr—"evolution" or change in form over time; impossible in the strictest interpretations of the immutable holy sources of Islam

Tawḥīd—the absolute unity and oneness of God, constituting an uncompro-ising monotheism

al-Ṭurābi, Hasan—leader of the National Islamic Front, formerly the Muslim Brotherhood, in Sudan; the principal architect of Islamic government and law and an international Islamist leader

'Ulamā'—official interpreters of the Sharī'a and holy sources of the religion; often associated with the power of the state

Umma—the world community of believers; a powerful transcultural, international identity of nearly one billion Muslims

'Umra—"visitation"; the lesser pilgrimage, lasting only four days

Urdu—language spoken in Islamic Pakistan, written in Arabic calligraphy

Usūl—foundation or fundamentals

Usūl al-Fiqh—foundations of Islamic jurisprudence

Usūliyya—"fundamentalism"

al-Wāli—the marriage guardian, usually the father, grandfather, uncle or other close male relation from among the 'asaba who insures that a woman marries well (to someone of equal standing)

Waqf, awqāf (pl.)—religious bequest for a charitable purpose, such as the support of a mosque, school, or hospital; cannot be altered or renegotiated once made

Zabalīn/zabaleen—Cairo trash and garbage collectors, dominated by Egyptian Copts; colloquial reference to the poor underclass

Zakāt—religiously inspired charitable donations, one of the five pillars of Islam; increasingly mandated as a tax as part of the drive toward Islamization of government

Zār—spirit possession cult outside of the formal practice of Islam; practiced by women in the Nile Valley, Ethiopia and across Saharan Africa, where it is also known as Bori cult

Zinjī, Zunūj (pl.)—refers to non-Arab, generally non-Muslim, Africans; may be used colloquially to refer to Negroes, or "blacks"; from *Zanjabar* or Zanzibar Island

Appendix B

Suggestions for Further Reading

Altorki, Soraya, and Camillia Fawzi El-Solh (eds.). 1988. *Arab Women in the Field: Studying Your Own Society*. Syracuse: Syracuse University Press.

Bates, D., and A. Rassam. 1983. *Peoples and Cultures of the Middle East*. Englewood Cliffs, N.J.: Prentice-Hall.

Beck, Lois, and Nikki Keddie (eds.). 1978. *Women in the Muslim World*. Cambridge: Harvard University Press.

Dwyer, Kevin. 1991. *Arab Voices: the Human Rights Debate in the Middle East*. Berkeley: University of California Press.

Eickelman, Dale F. 1989. *The Middle East: An Anthropological Approach*. 2d ed. Englewood Cliffs, N.J.: Prentice-Hall.

Eickelman, Dale F., and James Piscatori (eds.). 1990. *Muslim Travellers: Pilgrimage, Migration and the Religious Imagination*. Berkeley and Los Angeles: University of California Press.

Esposito, John L. 1990. *Islam, the Straight Path*. New York: Oxford University Press.

———. 1992. *The Islamic Threat: Myth or Reality?* New York: Oxford University Press.

Fernea, Elizabeth Warnock. 1965. *Guests of the Sheikh: An Ethnography of An Iraqi Village*. New York: Doubleday and Co.

Fernea, Elizabeth and Basima Bezirgan (eds.). 1977. *Middle Eastern Women Speak for Themselves*. Austin: University of Texas Press.

Fluehr-Lobban, Carolyn. 1987. *Islamic Law and Society in the Sudan*. London: Frank Cass and Co.

Gellner, Ernest. 1981. *Muslim Society*. Cambridge: Cambridge University Press.

Gilmore, David, 1987. *Honor and Shame and the Unity of the Mediterranean*. Special Publication no. 22, Washington, D.C.: American Anthropological Association.

Haddad, Yvonne Y. 1984. "Islam, Women and Revolution in Twentieth Century Arab Thought," *The Muslim World*, 74, nos. 3–4:137–60.

Haddad, Yvonne Yazbeck, and Adair T. Lummis. 1987. *Islamic Values in the United States: A Comparative Study*. New York: Oxford University Press.

Haddad, Yvonne Yazbeck, Byron Haines, and Ellison Findley (eds.). 1984. *The Islamic Impact*. Syracuse: Syracuse University Press.

Hourani, Albert. 1991. *History of the Arabs*. Cambridge, Mass.: Harvard University Press.

Hussain, Asaf, Robert Olson and Jamil Qureshi (eds.). 1984. *Orientalism, Islam and Islamists*. Brattleboro, Vt.: Amana Books.

Ibn Khaldun. 1981. *The Muqaddimah: An Introduction to History*. Translated from the Arabic by Franz Rosenthal. Edited and abridged by N. J. Dawood. Princeton, N.J.: Princeton University Press.

Kirtzeck, James. 1970. *Modern Islamic Literature, from 1800 to the Present*. New York: Holt, Rinehart and Winston.

Maalouf, Amin. 1984. *The Crusades Through Arab Eyes*. Translated by Jon Rothschild. Al Saqi Books, distributed by Zed Press, London.

Mahfouz, Naguib. 1981. *Children of Gebelawi*. Translated by Philip Stewart. Washington: Three Continents Press.

Malcolm X, with Alex Haley. 1992. *The Autobiography of Malcolm X*. New York: Ballantine Books. Originally published in 1964.

Nasr, Seyyad Hossein. 1987. *Traditional Islam in the Modern World*. London: Routledge and Kegan Paul.

Nyang, Sulayman S. 1984. *Islam, Christianity and African Identity*. Brattleboro, Vt.: Amana Books.

Pickthall, Mohammed Marmaduke. 1977. *The Meaning of the Glorious Qur'ān*. New York: The Muslim World League.

Rahman, Fazlur. 1979. *Islam*. 2d ed. Chicago: University of Chicago Press.

Rugh, Andrea B. 1984. *Family Life in Contemporary Egypt*. Syracuse: Syracuse University Press.

Said, Edward. 1978. *Orientalism*. New York: Pantheon Books.

———. 1981. *Covering Islam: How the Media Experts Determine How We See the Rest of the World*. New York: Pantheon Books.

Savory, R.M (ed.). 1989. *Introduction to Islamic Civilization*. Cambridge: Cambridge University Press.

Smith, Jane (ed.). 1980. *Women in Contemporary Muslim Society*. Lewisburg, Pa.: Bucknell University Press.

Toubia, Nahid (ed.) with an introduction by Nawal el-Saadawi. 1988. *Women of the Arab World, the Coming Challenge*. Translated by Nahed El Gamal. London: Zed Books.

Voll, John O. 1982. *Islam: Continuity and Change in the Modern World*. Boulder: Westview Press.

Recommended Journals

International Journal of Middle East Studies. Published by Cambridge University in association with the Middle East Studies Association.

Middle East Journal. Published by the Middle East Institute, Washington D.C.

Muslim World. Published by the Duncan Black Macdonald Center, Hartford Seminary.

References

Abdel Malik, Anour. 1963. "Orientalism in Crisis," *Diogenes,* 44:103–140.

Abu-Lughod, Janet. 1980. *Rabat, Urban Apartheid in Morocco.* Princeton: Princeton University Press.

Adams, William Y. 1984. *Nubia, Corridor to Africa.* Princeton: Princeton University Press.

Ali, General Fathi Ahmed (Commander-in-Chief of the Legitimate Command of the Sudanese Armed Forces). 1992. "Our Vision of the New Sudan".

Arnsten, Andrea. 1977. *Women and Social Change in Tunisia.* Ph.D. diss., Georgetown University.

Al-Ashmawy, Said. 1988–89. "Militant Doctrine in Islam." Paper presented at the American University in Cairo, Leiden University (Holland) and Rutgers University (US).

———. 1992. "Islamic Law and Human Rights". Unpublished paper, Cairo.

———. 1994. "Islam and the Political Order." Washington, D.C.: Council for Research in Values and Philosophy.

Beck, Lois and Nikki Keddie (eds.). 1978. *Women in the Muslim World.* Cambridge, Mass.: Harvard University Press.

Boddy, Janice. 1989. *Wombs and Alien Spirits: Men, Women and the Zār Cult in the Northern Sudan.* Madison: University of Wisconsin Press.

Coulson, N.J. 1971. *Succession in the Muslim Family.* Cambridge: Cambridge University Press.

Deng, Francis. 1989. *Cry of the Owl.* Boulder: Lynn Reiner.

Dwyer, Kevin. 1991. *Arab Voices: The Human Rights Debate in the Middle East.* Berkeley: University of California Press.

Eickelman, Dale. 1976. *Moroccan Islam.* Austin: University of Texas Press.

———. 1989. *The Middle East, An Anthropological Approach.* 2d ed. Englewood Cliffs, N.J.: Prentice-Hall.

Eickelman, Dale and James Piscatori (eds.). 1990. *Muslim Travellers: Pilgrimage, Migration and the Religious Imagination.* Berkeley: University of California Press.

Esposito, John L. 1982. *Women in Muslim Family Law.* Syracuse: Syracuse University Press.

———. 1988. *Islam, the Straight Path.* New York: Oxford University Press.

———. 1992. *The Islamic Threat: Myth or Reality?* New York: Oxford University Press.

Fernea, Elizabeth W. and Robert A. Fernea. 1991. *Nubian Ethnographies.* Prospect Heights, Ill.: Waveland Press.

Fluehr-Lobban, Carolyn. 1976. "An Analysis of Homicide in the Afro-Arab Sudan," *Journal of African Law,* 20, no. 1: 20–38.

———. 1977. "Agitation for Change in the Sudan," in *Sexual Stratification,* ed. A. Schlegel, pp. 127-143. New York: Columbia University Press.

———. 1981. "The Political Mobilization of Women in the Arab World," in *Women in Contemporary Muslim Society,* ed. Jane Smith, pp. 235–259. Lewisburg, Pa.: Bucknell University Press.

———. 1983. "Circulars of the Sharī'a Courts in the Sudan (Manshurāt El-Mahakim El-Sharī'a Fi Sudān) 1902–1979," *Journal of African Law,* 27, no. 2:79–140.

———. 1987. *Islamic Law and Society in the Sudan.* London: Frank Cass.

———. 1989. "Toward a Sudanese Law Appropriate to Majority and Minority Populations," *Law and Anthropology,* 4:187–200.

———. 1990. "Islamization in Sudan: A Critical Appraisal." *Middle East Journal,* 44, no. 4:610–623.

———. 1993. "Arab-Muslim Women as Activists in Secular and Religious Movements." *Arab Studies Quarterly* 15, no. 2: 87–106.

Fluehr-Lobban, C. and Lois Bardsley-Sirois. "Obedience (Ta'a) in Muslim Marriage: Religious Interpretation and Applied Law in Egypt." *Journal of Comparative Family Studies,* 21, 1:39–54.

Gellner, Ernest. 1981. *Muslim Society.* Cambridge: Cambridge University Press.

Gilmore, David. 1987. *Honor and Shame and the Unity of the Mediterranean.* Special Publication No. 22, Washington, D.C.: American Anthropological Association.

Grotberg, Edith and Sadiga Washi. 1991. "Critical Factors in Women's Status Predictive of Fertility Rates in the Sudan," Paper presented at the 11th annual conference of the Sudan Studies Association, Vassar College.

Haddad, Yvonne Y. 1984. "Islam, Women and Revolution in Twentieth Century Arab Thought," *Muslim World,* 74, nos. 3–4:137–60.

Handal, Najoua Kefi. 1989. *Islam and Political Development: The Tunisian Experience.* Ph.D. diss., Louisiana State University.

Hoffman-Ladd, Valerie. 1987. "Polemics on the Modesty and Segregation of Women in Contemporary Egypt," *International Journal of Middle East Studies,* 19:23–50.

Hourani, Albert. 1991. *The History of the Arabs.* Cambridge, Mass.: Harvard University Press.

Hussain, Afaf, Robert Olson, and Jamil Qureshi (eds.). 1984. *Orientalism, Islam and Islamists.* Brattleboro, Vt.: Amana Books.

Al-Jarida al-Rasmiyya (Official Gazette), no. 25 Supplement, 21 June, 1979, Cairo.

Jennings, Anne. 1989. *The Nubians of West Aswan.* Unpublished manuscript.

Kennedy, J. G. 1967. "Nubian Zār Ceremonies as Psychotherapy." *Human Organization,* 26: 185–194.

Kenyon, Susan. 1991. *Five Women of Sinnar*. Oxford: Clarendon Press.

Kerr, Malcolm H., and El Sayed Yassin (eds.). 1982. *Rich and Poor States in the Middle East: Egypt and the New Arab Order*. Boulder, Col.: Westview Press and the American University in Cairo Press.

Lerner, Gerda. 1986. *The Creation of Patriarchy*. New York: Oxford University Press.

Libidi, Lilia. 1987. *Al-Harikah al-Nisa' fi Tunis* (The Women's Movement in Tunisia). Tunis.

Lobban, Richard A. Jr. 1982. "Class and Kinship in Sudanese Urban Communities." *Africa* 52, no. 2:51–76.

———. 1993. "Pigs and Their Prohibition." *International Journal of Middle East Studies* 26, no. 1: in press.

Maalouf, Amin. 1984. *The Crusades Through Arab Eyes*. Translated by Jon Rothschild. Al Saqi Books, distributed by Zed Press, London.

Magnarella, Paul J. 1982. "The Republican Brothers: A Reformist Movement in the Sudan." *Muslim World* 72, no. 1: 14–21.

Magnuson, Douglas Kent. 1987. *Islamic Reform in Contemporary Tunisia, A Comparative Ethnographic Study*. Ph.D. diss., Brown University.

Mahfouz, Naguib. 1975. *Midaq Alley*. Translated by Trevor Le Gassick. London: Heinemann Educational Books.

Mahmoud, Mahgoub al-Tigani. 1992. "The Sudanese Fanatic Junta versus a New Alternative Sudan." African Centre for Democracy and Human Rights, Banjul, Gambia.

Mahmud, Ushari Ahmed, and Suleyman Ali Baldo. 1987. *Ed-Diein Massacre: Slavery in the Sudan*. Khartoum.

Malcolm X, with Alex Haley. 1992. *The Autobiography of Malcolm X*. New York: Ballantine Books. Originally published 1964.

Mernissi, Fatima. 1975. *Beyond the Veil: Male-Female Dynamics in Muslim Society*. Cambridge, Mass.: Schenkman Publishing Co.

Morgan, Robin, ed. 1984. *Sisterhood Is Global*. New York: Anchor Books.

Najjar, Fauzi M. 1986. "Egypt's Laws of Personal Status." Unpublished paper, revised version of a paper presented at 20th annual meeting of the Middle East Studies Association, Boston.

Nawwab, Ni'mah Isma'il. 1992. "The Journey of a Lifetime." *Aramco World Magazine* 43, no. 4:27–35.

Peristiany, J. G. (ed.). 1966. *Honor and Shame: The Values of Mediterranean Society*. Chicago: University of Chicago Press.

Peters, F.E. 1982. *Children of Abraham: Judaism/Christianity/Islam*. Princeton, N.J.: Princeton University Press.

Phillip, Thomas. 1978. "Feminism and Nationalist Politics in Egypt," in *Women in the Muslim World*, ed. Lois Beck and Nikki Keddie, pp. 277–94 Cambridge, Mass.: Harvard University Press.

Pickthall, Mohammed Marmaduke. 1977. *The Meaning of the Glorious Qur'ān*. New York: The Muslim World League.

References

Polk, William R., trans. 1974. *The Golden Ode by Labid Ibn Rabiah*. Cairo: The American University in Cairo Press.

El-Rasoul, Rawla Hasab. 1991. "Unifying the Application of Sharia," *Sudanow*, September: 29.

The Renaissance Party in Tunisia. 1991. *The Quest for Freedom and Democracy*. Washington, D.C.: AMC.

Rugh, Andrea. 1984. *Family Life in Contemporary Egypt*. Syracuse: Syracuse University Press.

El-Saadawi, Nawal. 1979. *The Hidden Face of Eve: Women in the Arab World*. London: Zed Press.

Said, Edward W. 1978. *Orientalism*. New York: Pantheon Books.

————. 1981. *Covering Islam*. New York: Pantheon Books.

Salacuse, Jeswald W. 1982. "Arab Capital and Trilateral Ventures in the Middle East: Is Three a Crowd?" In *Rich and Poor States in the Middle East*, ed. Malcolm H. Kerr and El Sayed Yassin, pp. 129–64. Boulder, Col.: Westview Press and American University in Cairo Press.

Schimmel, Annemarie. 1984. "Aspects of Mystical Thought in Islam." In *The Islamic Impact*, ed. Y. Haddad, B. Haines, and E. Findly, pp. 113–36. Syracuse: Syracuse University Press.

Shahin, Emad Eldin Ali. 1990. *The Restitution of Islam: A Comparative Study of the Islamic Movements in Contemporary Tunisia and Morocco*. Ph.D. diss., Johns Hopkins University.

Sherif-Stanford, Nahla. 1984. *Modernization by Decree: The Role of the Tunisian Woman in Development*. Ph.D. diss., University of Missouri–Columbia.

Sisk, Timothy D. 1992. *Islam and Democracy: Religion, Politics and Power in the Middle East*. Washington, D.C.: United States Institute for Peace.

Spaulding, Jay, and Lidwien Kapteijns. 1991. "The Orientalist Paradigm in the Historiography of the Late Precolonial Sudan," in *Golden Ages, Dark Ages: Imagining the Past in Anthropology and History*, ed. Jay O'Brien and William Roseberry, pp. 139–51. Berkeley: University of California Press.

Tessler, Mark A. 1978. "Women's Emancipation in Tunisia," in *Women in the Muslim World*, ed. L. Beck and N. Keddie, pp. 141–58. Cambridge, Mass.: Harvard University Press.

Tibawi, A. L. 1964. "English-Speaking Orientalists: A Critique of Their Approach to Islam and Arab Nationalism," *Islamic Quarterly* 8, pt. 1, nos. 1, 2: 24–44; pt. 2, nos. 3, 4:73–88.

Al-Turabi, Hasan. 1992. "Islam, Democracy, the State and the West". Lecture and Roundtable discussion at the University of South Florida, Tampa, May 10.

Waltz, Susan. 1988. "Self-Confidence, Determination, and Involvement in the Roots of Efficacy Among Women Political Leaders in Tunisia", Paper presented at the Arab-American University Graduates conference, San Francisco.

Index